P9-DMR-970

Praise for

★ "Eminently readable . . . This is an obvious complement to Palacio's *Wonder*, and it will be a gripping readaloud, readalone, and discussion point all on its own, too."

—*BCCB*, starred review

★ "Writing with humor, honesty, compassion, and grace . . . Hoge captures the nuances of his atypical experience . . . Hoge's parents' determination to provide him with as normal an upbringing as possible, combined with his own outgoing nature and desire to participate in all activities, makes his coming-of-age story unique and universal."

—*Publishers Weekly*, starred review

"In this honest, painful, and often funny memoir, readers will identify with Hoge's realization that everyone is different, and his are just 'different differences.'"

—*Booklist*

"The text is enormously accessible; Hoge draws readers in with creative language and analogies to help clarify and set the tone of his complex story . . . This empowering story will reach even the hardest of hearts. Recommended for its message of tolerance and acceptance." —*School Library Journal*

"Robert Hoge writes his exceptional life story in straightforward, compelling prose that forced me to question how often I judge what I see around me. Bravo, Mr. Hoge! Please write more books." —Holly Goldberg Sloan,
bestselling author of *Counting By 7s*

"*Ugly* made me think, it made me feel both joy and sadness, but most of all, it made me laugh. This is an honest, intelligent, and descriptive story of what it's like to grow up with a disability, including the good, the bad, and the . . . ugly."

—Shane Burcaw, author of *Laughing at My Nightmare*

"A jaw-dropping story of resilience, courage, and fierce hope."

—Joan Bauer, *New York Times*
bestselling author of *Almost Home*

ROBERT HOGE

UGLY

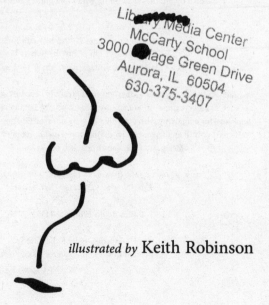

illustrated by **Keith Robinson**

Library Media Center
McCarty School
3000 Village Green Drive
Aurora, IL 60504
630-375-3407

3 0022 00512362 Q

PUFFIN BOOKS

PUFFIN BOOKS
An imprint of Penguin Random House LLC
375 Hudson Street
New York, New York 10014

First published by Hachette Australia, 2015
First published in the United States of America by Viking,
an imprint of Penguin Random House LLC, 2016
Published by Puffin Books, an imprint of Penguin Random House LLC, 2017

Text copyright © 2015, 2017 by Robert Hoge
Illustrations copyright © 2016 by Keith Robinson
Images copyright © 2017 by Robert Hoge
Vince / Mary / Robert image copyright © 1977 by News Ltd.

Penguin supports copyright. Copyright fuels creativity, encourages diverse voices, promotes
free speech, and creates a vibrant culture. Thank you for buying an authorized edition of this
book and for complying with copyright laws by not reproducing, scanning, or distributing
any part of it in any form without permission. You are supporting writers and allowing
Penguin to continue to publish books for every reader.

LIBRARY OF CONGRESS CATALOGING-IN-PUBLICATION DATA IS AVAILABLE.
ISBN: 9780425287750 (hardcover)

Puffin Books ISBN 9780425287774

Hand lettering by Kelley Brady
Printed in the United States of America

7 9 10 8

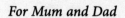
For Mum and Dad

Introduction

I guess you could call this the story of my story.

The proper "this is Robert's big, exciting life of ugliness" story starts just a couple of pages beyond this. But I wanted to write an introduction for this special edition of *Ugly* to tell you some of the reasons why I wrote the book. If you'd rather skip ahead and read about my actual life first, that's fine. This will be here when you finish. I'll wait.

When I was growing up, I had no idea that I would ever have a story worth telling, let alone one people might want to read or listen to. First of all, there was just too much life to be living—making new friends, fighting with my brothers and sisters, wondering if I'd ever make it onto the football team, and getting into mischief. Beneath those parts of my childhood, though, the ugly little pieces of my story were falling into place.

Eventually, my life became my story. And I decided there were more reasons to write *Ugly* than to leave it unwritten.

The first reason was the simplest: I love telling stories. Storytelling is the Krazy Glue that holds us all together. Stories can soar and sing and surprise. And sometimes, when we share our own stories, they do all three at once.

My story certainly had a surprising start. I was born with a massive tumor in the middle of my face and two deformed legs. My parents weren't initially sure what to do with me, and my doctors didn't even know if I'd live very long. Understanding my parents' initial feelings and sharing a little bit of their story with others who may have faced a similar situation was the second major reason for writing my story.

The final reason I wrote *Ugly* is the most important. I wanted to talk to you, readers, about what it means to grow up looking and feeling different. Too often, adults try to suggest that differences in appearance don't matter by pretending they simply don't exist. But you and I know the world looks different. Why? Because *we* are different. We don't have to define ourselves solely by our differences, but we don't have to ignore them, either.

It's also worth saying that most books are a little bit of a lie— even when the story they're telling is true.

Lives in books often look like a completed jigsaw puzzle. Even if the puzzle was messy to start with, by the end of a book all the pieces magically fall into place. Like puzzle pieces, lives in books have some sharp corners, some curvy parts, and some straight edges. One piece clicks into another, and the picture they make becomes clear and complete.

When you're in the middle of actually living your life, however, there's no picture of what it should look like at the end to guide your choices.

Few people know what the big picture of their life is going to look like while they're living it. I certainly didn't when I was growing up. I questioned a lot of my choices and often wondered if I had done the right thing. The answers only seem obvious when you get to the end of the book, when you turn the last page and the puzzle suddenly looks complete.

Life is not a book, though.

If you're different from other kids, don't worry about the jigsaw puzzle. Don't judge yourself by everyone else's seemingly beautiful picture. And don't worry if your final picture doesn't seem clear or if the edges around your story don't seem sharp. It might become clear later. Maybe it will remain entirely random until the very last piece slots into place, when everything becomes beautifully obvious. Or maybe the puzzle pieces won't ever seem to entirely fit together at all.

All of that's okay. None of us knows which bits of our lives will slot nicely together while we are living them. We are all a bit worried sometimes, confused at other times—even if our books make our lives seem magical.

The solution is simple: Be unafraid of living.

The puzzles pieces will take care of themselves.

1

The Art of Being Ugly

Imagine you're in art class. The teacher drops a lump of wet, sticky clay on the bench in front of you.

"You've got thirty minutes to sculpt a newborn baby's face," she says.

Everyone in the class waits, wondering if there are more instructions to come.

"Go!"

You grab the lump of clay and try to figure out where to start. First, better get the size right. You start tearing big chunks of clay off until the size looks okay and then you tackle the overall shape. There's a big bulge on one side that you need to press hard with the palm of your hand to fix.

When that looks about right, you shape the face itself and smooth the forehead. Next you craft a chin and push the clay with your thumb to add a little dimple. As you start to sculpt details—soft cheeks, a lovely small nose, perfect ears, eyes that are closed because you decide this newborn baby is asleep—you realize your sculpture is coming together just right.

"Time's almost up," your teacher says.

Your hands are racing across the clay. You've got just enough time to finish a few special touches, like eyebrows and a wisp of hair on top of the baby's head.

There's grit under your fingernails and your hands are sticky from the clay, but it doesn't matter. You look down and see a beautiful day-old baby in front of you. This is going to be an A+ assignment.

Then, out of the corner of your eye, you see someone running toward you. It's that one kid in class who really hates you. Yep, that one. Turns out he's so jealous of how good a job you've done that he rushes toward your sculpture. You reach out to stop him, but it's too late. He shoves a ball of clay right in the middle of the face you've made. You hear a soft squelch and then gasp as you see the damage the attack has done.

Your sculpture looks ruined. The little nose you made has been squashed by a giant clay splotch spread across the face. It has been pushed so hard into the face that the beautiful eyes you made are now way farther apart than they should be. The extra time you'd put into getting the size and shape of the head just right is totally wasted too. It's bumpy and broken.

Imagine what that sculpture looks like now, and you'll know what I looked like when I was born.

I'm the ugliest person you've never met.

It wasn't supposed to be that way. No one had any idea what was coming. My parents had four children before me, and I should have been born, plain and simple. On a Friday. But July 21, 1972, came—and almost went—without much to show for it.

As midnight neared, however, my mother, Mary Hoge, went into labor. My parents didn't own a telephone, so Mom rushed next door and asked the neighbors to call my father, Vince, home from work. Dad raced back from his job at a factory that made food for chickens. They had no time to spare. It would take them about half an hour to reach the hospital from our suburban Brisbane home.

My father arrived, jumped out of the car into the dark night, and ran upstairs. He packed my mother into the car as fast as he could, and they left for the hospital.

When Mom was admitted, her contractions that signaled the baby was coming were two minutes apart. Her baby should be there very soon. But at 2 a.m. on Saturday morning the contractions stopped dead. The doctors were worried and told my parents they might have to induce labor if the contractions didn't restart. Mom was sent to the hospital ward to wait. At 5:30 a.m. on Sunday, July 23, her contractions resumed. It was a long, difficult labor for a fifth baby, and I was born at 12:35 p.m.

Back then, a mother's usual first question would have been: "Is it a boy or a girl?" But something didn't seem quite right, so my mother had a different question for the doctors.

"Is my baby okay?" she asked.

"No, Mrs. Hoge," the doctor said, looking up in shock. "He is not okay. He has a lump on his head, and something wrong with his legs."

The lump was a massive bulge that jutted out from the top of my forehead and ran all the way down to the tip of where my nose should have been. It was almost twice the size of my newborn fist. It had formed early during my development and made a mess of my face, pushing my eyes to either side of my head. Like a fish.

That wasn't all. Looking down at me, the doctors saw that both my legs were mangled. The right leg was only three-quarters as long as it should have been and had a small foot bent forward at a very strange angle. The foot had four toes, and two of them were partially joined together. My left leg was even shorter and only had two toes. Both looked bent and broken.

I didn't get a hug from Mom before she sent me away, but I did get a name before she'd even laid eyes on me: Robert Vincent Hoge.

Dad had already visited me on his own by the time he saw Mom. When he described how I looked, they both burst into tears.

"Perhaps he'll die," Mary said to her husband.

Growing up on his parents' farm, Vince had birthed plenty of calves and lambs. He knew I might be an ugly baby, a baby with a tremendous number of problems, but he also knew his son was a fighter.

"No chance—he's too strong and healthy," he said.

That didn't stop my mother feeling awful about it all, though. The next day was her birthday, and she'd expected a perfect baby as the best present ever. Instead, she got a little monster. I was sent to the hospital's intensive-care ward—ugly and alone.

2

Left Behind

As soon as I arrived at the intensive-care ward, doctors started lots of medical tests. They attached me to machines to check my breathing and my heart rate. They poked and prodded my body to try to find out if all my internal organs were where they should be. Then they started trying to work out if I could see and hear, and if my brain was damaged.

One thing they rushed to discover was whether my deformities were blocking the flow of fluid that helps cushion the spine and brain. If that happened, my head would swell up like a balloon and I would die in a few days. There would be no way of fixing it.

Doctors at the hospital answered most of those questions quickly. There were no problems with my heart or lungs or other internal organs that they could see. All my mysteries were written on the outside of my body. Why did I have a massive tumor squished across my face? Why were my legs deformed? Would I be able to walk?

I was also the subject of a lot of questions people were asking my mother. Everyone wanted to know when she would come and see me. Every time she was asked if she wanted to leave the mothers' ward to go see her baby in intensive care, her answer was the same: no.

"I wished he would go away or die or something," Mom explained later, when she started writing some of her thoughts down.

Worse than that, Mom had decided she wanted to leave me in the hospital.

"I just wanted to be finished with it all," she said. "I told the hospital staff I didn't want my baby. I wouldn't under any circumstances take *it* home."

There were other normal kids at home to think about, after all—my brothers and sisters. Dad was at home looking after them. Michael was just four days away from turning ten when I was born, Gary was eight, Paula seven, and Catherine four.

Dad told them about me.

"The new baby is a boy," he said. "But he has some health problems and may not live long."

They asked what was wrong with me.

"He's got problems with his face, and his legs are small and not properly formed," Dad said.

"But he's only a baby yet and they will grow," Michael said.

"That's not how it works, Michael," Dad told him.

After I'd been in the intensive-care ward for about a week, one of the doctors visiting Mom sensed something different about the way she was feeling. The doctor asked my mother if she would finally like to see her baby.

Mom knew there was something terribly wrong with me. Until she saw me, though, the pain and grief only needed to exist in her mind. Her feelings were real enough, but with an unseen, distant cause. If she pretended I didn't exist, maybe those bad feelings would just go away. But before she'd thought it through, Mom said yes, she'd go see me.

Together, she and the doctor walked to my ward. Mom slowed down as she got closer and closer, not knowing exactly what to expect. The doctors and my dad had described me to her, but she still hadn't seen me with her own eyes. Not even a photograph. She walked into my ward and saw other normal-looking babies in their small cots. The doctor guided my mother over to where I was.

My mother looked down on me for the first time and saw the large tumor that had robbed her of a baby's perfection. She saw my too widely spread eyes and my splayed nostrils. She saw my deformed legs and bent toes.

Mom looked at me again and decided she did not care about her son. About me.

"I didn't feel anything for this baby," she wrote in her diary. "I had shut off completely. I had made up my mind I was not taking him home."

She packed her bags and left the hospital without me.

I had my first operation when I was five days old. Surgeon Leigh Atkinson operated to see what was behind the tumor that had caused so many problems with my face.

Afterward he told my parents my brain seemed okay and I should have a normal life span.

Medical staff then began to tell Mom about advances in surgical procedures.

"There's so much more that can be done these days," a nurse told her.

"We can do a lot to help fix Robert," another surgeon said.

They were not the words a mother who had just given birth wanted to hear. Mom began phoning anyone she thought might help her refuse to take me. She called her member of parliament and then her local doctor. The doctor's advice was very clear.

"Put him into a home," the doctor said. "You have four other children and it's just not worth it."

She asked whether he could make that sort of judgment without having even seen me.

"Yes," he said. "No doubt he would be better off in a home. Don't even consider bringing him home. Just forget him."

My father figured Mom should be the one to decide, since she'd be looking after me most of the time.

"You'll have my full support, whatever decision you make," Dad said.

The hospital made an appointment for Mom to meet with a social worker and discuss the situation. Mom didn't show up. I remained in the hospital, unwanted and unloved.

Mom started to visit more often, but she was still terribly unhappy and couldn't bring herself to take me home. One day, after a visit, she cried and told her sister in a moment of desperation and honesty, "He is so ugly."

Mom kept asking other people what she should do. No one gave her an answer. They all said the same thing: it was her decision and they would support her whatever she did.

Over the next few weeks, she realized she had to approach the situation more rationally. She had to think the issues through, address them, and then decide. It was a decision that would affect the whole family, every aspect of their lives, for a very long time.

Finally, Dad and Mom agreed they should explain to my brothers and sisters exactly what was wrong with me and give everyone a chance to have their say.

One Saturday morning my parents sat down with their four older children and had a family discussion. They explained the situation, describing what I looked like

and what was wrong with my legs. They talked for a long time and when they finished the whole family was crying. Then came the big question.

Mom pointed at my eldest brother, Michael, and asked, "Should we bring Robert home?"

Michael paused, silent for a few seconds while everyone watched and waited.

"Yes," he said.

"And you?" Mom asked, and pointed at Gary.

"Yes," Gary said.

Then came Paula. "Yes," she said.

Finally, Mom pointed at Catherine.

"Should we bring Robert home?" Mom asked.

Catherine paused.

"Yes," Catherine said, but she was only four years old and mostly thought she should say "yes" because that's what everyone else had said first.

A few days after that, the whole family came to visit me in the hospital and my brothers and sisters each had a turn holding me. Not one of them changed their mind about bringing me home. There was concern and curiosity on their young faces, but all of it was for me, not for themselves.

My sister Paula doesn't remember the way I looked being a major issue for my siblings when I first came home. "You were a baby and it was just the way you were," she said.

Mom started to understand that she had been focusing on what other people might think of her new baby.

"My worry and my concern were more a matter of pride than anything else," Mom said.

She started thinking about how she might have reacted if my problems were on the inside rather than the outside.

"If Robert had serious medical problems within, I would never have hesitated to accept him, but because he looked different I found it so terribly hard," she said later.

Mom realized it wouldn't be the last tough decision she would have to make about my future. It was not going to be easy. She knew it would mean battles for her and for me, but she had made up her mind.

It was August 28, 1972—a month and five days after I had been born. I was finally going home.

3

Home

If our house was a dog it would be a rough little mongrel of a thing—not big, not fancy, not pretty. Luckily it was a happy mutt most of the time.

The tiny timber place my parents owned was typical of the Brisbane, Australia, seaside suburb they lived in. The front door opened into a small lounge room. On the right was a row of tall, narrow windows that were wedged open all year, save for a few cold weeks in winter and the occasional summer storm. Past that was the kitchen with its sink, stove, and a brown table that sagged in the middle. A skinny hallway ran alongside the lounge room joining it to three bedrooms, the toilet, and the bathroom. That was it, as far as inside went at least.

Outside, the yard was an ocean of green grass, punctuated only by a clothesline, a barbecue, a hedge along one fence, and an assortment of fruit trees and vegetable patches.

A man's home might be his castle, but the four fences of that yard became my mother's prison. After fighting so long to keep from bringing me home, Mom was reluctant to take me out again once she did. She was not ready to face the verdict of strangers when they saw her strange child. For a long time, the only place I went as a baby was to the hospital for various appointments. No shopping trips. No playground visits. Just appointments and Fortress Hoge.

The hospital wasn't always a safe place, though. Even there, people were ready to make assumptions about me based on how I looked. One time before an appointment, Mom left me with Dad while she went to make a phone call. Two women stood in line in front of her waiting to use the phone.

"He comes up here often," one said to the other, looking toward me.

"Really?"

"Yes, he's got deformed legs, a harelip, and a cleft palate and is not normal mentally. . . ."

A harelip and cleft palate were often related and occurred when a problem during pregnancy meant a baby's lip and the roof of his or her mouth didn't join together properly.

Mom spun around.

"That is my son you are discussing," she hissed at them.

The women looked at her in surprise.

"He has not got a harelip or a cleft palate and he is quite normal mentally," Mom said. "And I'll thank you not to make a diagnosis until you are more qualified."

They turned away without saying anything.

It might have taken her a week to come and see me for the first time and another month before she decided to bring me home, but when she did, Mom's love for me grew fast and fierce.

A few months later, Mom decided she was ready to take me into the big wide world. Like countless other moms and their kids had done before, we went for a trip to the local shops. Expecting the worst, she held her head high to avoid meeting the gaze of other shoppers, but no one commented, and if anyone stared at me, she didn't notice. In the future, whenever she did find people staring at her and her ugly little boy, Mom settled for staring back.

Dad approached things differently. He was tall, with broad shoulders, and hair cropped so close to his head it made his giant ears stick out even more. He was pretty rough-and-ready himself and had no problems taking me out in public. He mostly ignored adults when they stared, or told them, "Pull your head in." With kids, he took a less direct approach.

Sometimes, when I was old enough, we'd swim at the Wynnum Wading Pool—a massive ocean pool on the coast fed by the water coming in at high tide. Local legend had it you couldn't take three paces without stepping on broken glass, dog poo, or a rusty piece of the pool's slippery metal slide that had flaked away.

"You shouldn't go swimming in it," a kid told me once.

"Why not?" I asked.

"A baby shark swam through the grates and has grown and grown and is now big enough to eat you," the boy said, and he made a chomping motion with his arms.

I wasn't sure at first, but decided to take my chances.

I couldn't hide my face when I was swimming, or the fact I didn't have normal legs, so once in a while I'd hear comments or get questions.

"Look at his legs!" "Why do you have a squashed nose?" "What's wrong with your face?" I'd either try to ignore them or reply, "Nothing." Not Dad, though. If he was in hearing distance when a child came to stare and ask a pointed question, he'd yell, "Oi, you! Go tell your mother she wants you."

One time when Dad yelled that at a boy who'd asked me if I could smell through my nose, the boy replied, "But I don't have a mother."

"Must have been your father, then," Dad said.

While my parents started to figure out how I might fit into the world as I was, doctors at the Mater Children's Hospital were thinking about how they could help me fit in better.

This meant tests and appointments with every kind of medical professional possible: face doctors, brain doctors, speech therapists, eye doctors, dentists, leg doctors, doctors who helped people move around better, and doctors whose job it was to keep you mentally fit and happy.

So. Many. Doctors.

The first thing they decided to do was to chop off part of one of my legs. The doctors told my parents I'd never walk on my squished left leg normally. It was just too short. That meant amputating the foot and the bottom of the leg, and fitting me with a prosthesis—an artificial leg.

The leg had a leather socket that covered my stump. It was attached like a shoe—there was a split down the middle with a long lace pulled tight through holes on either side. To wear it, I'd pull a thick woolen sock over my real leg, slip the fake one over it and tighten the lace so it didn't fall off. Two metal strips ran from the bottom of the socket all the way down to a circular lump of metal about an inch and a half thick that rested on the ground. My new foot.

What to do about my right leg was more complicated. The foot on it was angled forward like a ballerina's pointed toes. I could put the front of my foot on the ground when I stood up but not the heel. An operation to fix it failed.

Mom and Dad tried to get a special boot made that would fit my foot—a high heel for a two-year-old boy—but that didn't work either. By the time I turned two years old, I still couldn't walk.

My parents kept trying, though. After another year of

slow and patient practice, one day my mom took me by the arms and helped me up our front stairs. On the landing she stood me up and got me to hold on to the railing. She took a few steps backward and held out her hands.

"Walk to me, Robert," she said.

I was nervous and stayed holding on to the railing.

"You can do it," she said.

Slowly I took a step toward her, then another. And then I fell over.

"Well done, Robert," Mom said.

Then she got me to do it again. I did. When my brothers and sisters came home from school I did it for them too. Finally, Dad returned home from work. He came and sat in the lounge room and Mom held me up between her outstretched hands.

"Walk to Daddy," she whispered in my ear.

I took a tentative step after she let go of my hands and didn't fall over. Then I took another step and another, before making it all the way over to my father.

I was three years old and had just taken my first steps.

It's probably no surprise that my earliest memory is about being in the hospital. After the surgery on my right ankle, I had a plaster cast covering my leg. One of the nurses put me on the floor to play and I apparently sat for a little while, then took off.

I remember crawling up a set of stairs bathed in sunlight. They looked like giant chocolate bars stacked on top of each other. I found my way into a strange room that had a long center aisle with a shiny floor and long, flat seats on either side. There were colorful windows and unusual paintings on the wall. Someone was sitting, alone and quiet, down in the front of the room.

I had found my way into the hospital's chapel, one floor up from my hospital ward.

I clomped toward the front of the room, the plaster cast on my leg banging on the wooden floor as I crawled. The nun remained still for a moment, then turned with a kind of dread in her eyes. I think she prayed a little bit harder hearing me coming up behind her.

By the time I turned three, my doctors recommended that I undergo a major operation to fix my face. My facial deformities didn't present an ongoing danger to my physical health, but the doctors were concerned that they might make it hard for me to make friends.

Despite the love of a mother and a father for their son, despite my general health and well-being, I was still ugly. Not just plain ugly either. Mine wasn't any sort of cheap, home-brand ugly—it was an A-grade, top-of-the-range ugly.

The doctors wanted to make me a friend-friendly face.

Before they went too far with their planning, however, Dr. Atkinson asked that I have a more intense mental evaluation. Were I intellectually disabled too, they probably wouldn't have gone ahead. Fortunately, I met all of my mental-development milestones, and a test showed I was smart enough to make all the effort worthwhile.

The operation they proposed was a major one. It would make medical history, they said. It would change my life forever, they said.

Or end it.

4

Hide-and-Seek

Pick up two dice.

Now roll them.

If the number rolled adds up to ten, eleven, or twelve, I die on the operating table.

That's essentially what the doctors at the Mater hospital told my parents when they discussed the operation they were planning.

"The operation is crucial," one doctor said.

"It's vital in ways that go beyond your son's physical health," another said. "Please understand, though, there's a significant chance Robert could die while we're operating."

Humans are like social Legos. We connect together with families. We build lives with friends. On our own, we're just one piece. When we come together in groups, we make amazing things. Our admission ticket into these groups is not our thoughts or our feelings. Our faces are our tickets. Our faces let us look out and know others and let them know us.

Doctors had done a small operation just after I was born to remove the tumor that split the middle of my face and caused my facial deformities. It meant I was left with no nose at all—and with nostrils drilled into the flat center of my face. Plus, my eyes still sat more than twice as far apart as they should have been.

They were so far apart I couldn't use both of them to focus on any one thing at the same time. If I wanted to look closely at something like a toy or a book, I either had to pick it up and move it around to the side of my head or turn my head to bring one eye in line with it. It also meant I couldn't judge distances properly. Without this depth perception I wouldn't be able to catch a ball and I would forever be walking into walls.

The doctors were worried my face would prove a huge problem when I ventured beyond the safe walls of Fortress

Hoge and into the big, wide world. They were concerned that my stand-out-in-a-crowd face might make me afraid to go out in public, let alone do things like talk to people. Without some facial surgery, I might play the perfect game of hide-and-seek—never emerging to make friends.

Any surgery would need to be done well before I started school, to give me time to recover. But the bone structure in a baby's head is as chaotic as a busy road during peak hour. Bone plates move and grow over time, with the skull eventually forming a thick, solid layer of protection around the brain. Any operations done on my bones might stop them growing properly and mean the whole thing would fail.

The doctors decided the best time to operate would be when I was about four and a half years old. By then the underlying structure of my face would be set and I'd have plenty of time to recover before school.

Slowly and surely the doctors drew their plans to carve up my cranium, move some pieces around, toss away the chunks they didn't need, and put some new stuff in for good measure. They'd move my eyes closer together, reposition my nostrils and build me a new nose from the ground up. All that medical magic would give me a new face that was more acceptable to society.

But the magic trick came with a catch.

It was major surgery: a type of operation hardly ever performed anywhere in the world, let alone a nation as small as Australia. The doctors could not be sure how long the intricate surgery would take, but they were expecting it would be up to six hours. That meant lots of risks.

Being put under general anesthetic for so long presents a risk of brain damage. Next up was the chance of infection, which is especially high when bone is being cut and moved around. Any operation on the face also means lots of bleeding. Combined, the risks meant the operation could kill me.

"The chance of Robert dying while we operate is as high as one in four," the doctors said.

I'd had six operations since I was born, but none was anywhere near as risky as this one.

To complicate things even more, my doctors told Mom and Dad they wanted to amputate my right foot at the same time. It was a sad blow. An operation on my right ankle hadn't worked. The doctors said I'd be better off with two artificial legs rather than having just one and a deformed foot that didn't reach the ground properly. Instead of just disposing of the foot, though, the doctors wanted to use cartilage from the toes to build me a new nose.

The doctors put the question to my parents. Given all the benefits, and all the risks, would they give the go-ahead for the surgery?

Dad was a gambler and understood the odds the doctors gave him. He didn't want to roll those dice.

"No," he said. "No operation to make Robert look better is worth a one-in-four chance of him dying."

"Why not?" Mom asked.

Dad told her he was never one to be concerned about "pride of appearance," as he called it. What use was there in being slightly less ugly and dead?

Mom wanted to go ahead despite the risks. She thought it needed to be done to give me a fair chance at a normal social life. My parents argued back and forth. For months the question remained unresolved. With the help of the doctors, Mom mounted a strong case and moved Dad from a definite "no" to a "probably not."

But he'd go no further. Eventually the issue came to a head. The hospital only needed the signature of one parent to do the surgery. Mom told Dad that if he said no, she would consider leaving him and taking me with her so the decision would be all hers.

She had gone from being a new mother who did not want to see her baby, let alone bring him home, to someone who would put everything on the line for his future. Mom wasn't trying to blackmail Dad. She was just showing him how strongly she believed that the operation was worth the risk. Blackmail wouldn't have worked on Dad anyway.

A few days later Dad finally said yes. Even though he couldn't understand why people would judge others at face value, he knew it was a fact of life. To be fair to me, he said, to save me from being rejected by society, the operation should go ahead. Both Mom and Dad signed the consent form.

Those dice were about to be rolled.

5

The Big Fix

Remember the baby's head sculpture you did in our imaginary art class? Dig it out. Not the nice, A+ one you started with, mind you. No, we need the ugly, bumpy one with the squished nose you had at the end of it all.

"Make it normal," your teacher says.

This time you don't waste a moment waiting for more instructions.

Looking at it, you see right away that the biggest problem is the massive chunk of clay in the middle of the face that's not supposed to be there. You start trying to reshape the nose and smooth over some of the bumps, but the clay has started to harden and it's a lot more difficult to work with. It doesn't move so easily beneath your hands now. Pretty quickly you figure out that working only on the outside isn't going to be enough. You might be able to smooth the skin a bit, but there's still a big mess in the middle of the face, and the eyes are nowhere near where they should be.

If just working on the outside won't fix it, you think, maybe you can work from the inside out instead.

You gouge away the big chunk that's not supposed to be there and then dig some clay out of the very middle of the face. As you push the sides back together, the eyes move closer to where they should be. After that you can smooth out a few bumps. But your sculpture still needs a nose, so you grab some of the clay you set aside before and make a new one. Carefully you place it on the front of the face where the nose should be. Done.

That's what my doctors had to do to my face.

The operation took more than a year to plan. Heading the team were the doctor who had spent the most time talking to my parents after I was born, Dr. Atkinson, and plastic surgeon Dr. Tony Emmett. They had years and years of experience between them, but they still had a lot to learn before they would be ready. The type of operation they were planning was only just starting to prove successful overseas, in Mexico and in France.

The doctors took trips to France, the United States, Scotland, and Mexico to study new techniques that were being developed—especially those of French surgeon Paul Tessier, whose pioneering work was fundamental. Dr. Tessier's approach was a bold one. Before then, patients with complex facial problems like mine had different parts of their faces treated separately. Doctors would fix one part of the jigsaw, then the next and the next and the next.

Dr. Tessier's suggestion was that you get all the experts together to try to fix as many of the problems as they could all at once. Fewer operations meant better results and reduced the likelihood of complications. The technique was called craniofacial surgery. Improvements in anesthetics, and new drills and bone saws that allowed for precision cutting of the skull, made it possible.

The surgical team took life-size pictures of my face and X-rays of my skull so they could match the two together and see where bone and skin would have to be cut and moved. To rehearse and refine the procedure, Dr. Atkinson and Dr. Emmett took human skulls home at night and practiced cutting them up.

When everything was ready, the plan included forty different surgical procedures. They just needed a team to do it. Then, like superhero Avengers, the team assembled at Mater: five surgeons who'd work on different parts of my body, two assistants to help them, three anesthetists to make sure I stayed unconscious during the operation, plus nine different nurses. And me, the Hulk.

Teams started work at both ends of my body at the same time. One surgeon amputated my right foot and the bottom of my leg, while at the other end the doctors started remaking my face. They cut through the top of my skull so they would have easier access to my eye sockets and could move skin and bone around more accurately.

The surgeons carefully cut around the bones of my eye sockets and moved each eye a little more than half an inch—from the side of my head to the front, and down slightly. They had to leave room to build my nose, but the eye surgeon made sure the sockets were as close to where they should be as possible.

The whole time, doctors had to pump blood into me to replace what I was losing.

The surgeons who had amputated my leg were now working on the skin, bone, and cartilage they had removed. They used a long part of the bone from my amputated big toe to make a bridge for my new nose. Then they took cartilage from the amputated foot and sculpted it around the bone to make me a nose. Leftover bone was used to fill the large gaps where my eye sockets had originally been.

It sounds simple, but the whole procedure took double the time expected, clocking in at more than twelve hours.

I started the day as a boy with a right leg and deformed foot, no nose, and eyes at the sides of my head. I finished it with eyes at the front of my head, no right leg, no foot, and a new nose. I'd had my leg cut off and my head cut open and put back together again. I'd been under anesthetic for a dangerously long time. My blood had been replaced three times over. Despite all this, I survived.

I was Robert Hoge, born a second time.

6

A Different Little Boy

I emerged from the operation a very different little boy.

In Mater's intensive-care unit I was hooked up to life support to make sure my heart kept beating and my lungs kept breathing. I progressed well for the first few days, until my kidneys started malfunctioning. The kidneys are the umpires of the body. They regulate lots of its functions—filtering blood, producing hormones, helping to control blood pressure, and removing waste from the body.

My kidneys were blowing the whistle on my body.

The doctors warned Mom and Dad I might have to be put on kidney dialysis. My parents waited nervously as the doctors tried every trick they knew. Perhaps my kidneys were listening in, though, because just in time, they started working properly again.

"When will Robert be out of danger?" Mom asked a few days after the surgery.

"Each day, one more danger is eliminated," Dr. Atkinson said. There were plenty more days left.

Although I was still groggy when I came out of the operating room, I had managed to squeeze Mom's finger to tell her I was okay. But I had been kept under heavy sedation for the first few days and hadn't managed to speak to my parents. On arriving for a visit one day, Mom was told I had spoken my first words since the procedure.

Deep down Mom was probably hoping for something profound or sweet—maybe "I'm alive" or "Where's Mommy?"

"What did he say?" Mom asked the nurse.

"I want to do a poo," she replied. It wasn't very exciting, but it was what I always said when I wanted to use the toilet. It was a sign I probably hadn't suffered brain damage during the half day on the operating table.

When the doctors took my bandages off, they discovered I'd been replaced by a small, ugly alien. All my messy, sandy-brown hair was gone and in its place was reddened and raw skin. I had long lines of ragged stitches holding the skin together across the top of my head and down the middle of my face, right over the center of my new nose. I had two huge, swollen black eyes. Plastic tubes hung out of each nostril, draining phlegm and mucus.

Despite all the mess, the doctors looked at me and smiled. They had done what they'd set out to do. My face wasn't perfect, but the building blocks were better. Techniques the doctors had pioneered on me would later be used to help hundreds of other patients around Australia and the world.

Nothing comes without a cost, though.

My left eye was slightly damaged when it was moved, leaving the vision permanently blurred. Doctors tried to correct it with glasses, but had no luck. Still, it was a small price to pay for better depth perception.

The doctors told Mom and Dad they wanted to operate again in the future, but the hard work had been done. Future operations would do even more to improve my looks—fix up the bumps and scars they had been unable to remedy this time.

I left the hospital three weeks after the operation.

Around the same time, Mom was contacted to see if she and Dad would be interested in having a journalist from the *Australian*, a newspaper, do a story on me and the operation. They spent some time thinking it over. Mom and Dad weren't sure at first, but two things swayed them in the end.

The first was that they wanted the doctors and medical staff who had performed the operation, and all of the staff at the hospital, to receive some recognition for their efforts. The second and more important reason, from their perspective, was that they thought my story might help someone else. Maybe there were parents like them who had a child like me, who needed a gentle tap on the shoulder and someone to tell them there was hope.

After meeting my parents and me, and talking to the doctors responsible, journalist Hugh Lunn wrote a feature that was published in the newspaper in May 1977. The story talked about my birth and my parents' roller coaster of emotions, but focused mainly on the planning of the operation and the procedure itself. All the details of the surgery were spelled out, including the doctors' wonderful ingenuity in making me a new nose out of my toe.

When I had been home from the hospital for six weeks, I developed what at first seemed like a slight infection. I was readmitted to Mater for observation. The infection proved to be decidedly stubborn. The doctors became increasingly worried, and I ended up spending five long months in the hospital while they tried to beat it. As a child, it seemed like an eternity—but at least it was a familiar environment. Every time I went to the hospital, I'd stay in the same ward, often in the same bed, and while some of the doctors and nurses and ward staff caring for me came and went, most of the faces remained the same.

Mom would visit every day during the week. She'd arrive and give me a hug. The necklace she often wore—a large coin with Queen Victoria set in silver on one side—would brush across my forehead as she bent down. She would sit with me and we'd play and read together. Then she would wander the ward, talking to nurses and other regular patients.

Dad would visit on Saturday while Mom stayed home and made cupcakes—usually with help from Paula and Catherine. On Sunday the whole family came to visit. Mom would distribute the cakes she'd made the day before to the other sick children—some for the boys' ward and some for the girls'.

With my right leg amputated, I had to learn how to get around with no legs. It wasn't hard. Getting around without artificial legs was a joyous freedom. I no longer had a leg that got in the way. I could crawl or raise myself up on both arms and swing my body forward underneath me. And I could leap—onto couches, off beds, down stairs. I was fast in a way I never had been before.

Then I had an artificial leg made and fitted for my right stump. It was a lot easier to keep on than my left. It hugged tightly to my stump and was held on with a strap above my knee. Once it was all ready, I had to learn to walk on two artificial legs.

Imagine putting on shoes that have big heels on them. Then imagine getting six cans of soda and stacking them in two towers close to each other. Now imagine trying to stand on top of those two towers of soda cans and balance in your big shoes. That's what it felt like the first time I stood up with two artificial legs on. It was hard to balance, and I had to hang on to a railing for support. As soon as I let go, I'd feel my hips start to wobble and then I'd fall over—like a stack of books piled too high.

It was even worse when I tried to walk. I'd put one foot

down and start walking, then I'd sway to one side. Immediately I'd try to fix it by shifting my weight to the other side, but often I'd go too far and overbalance. Pretty quickly I became an expert at falling down, shoving my hands in front of me so I didn't smash my already ugly face into the ground. Each time I'd manage a few more steps before falling over, and eventually I got the hang of it.

It was perfect timing, because I'd be off to school in a few short months. Mom had no intention of sending me to a school for the disabled, even though she was constantly asked if that's where I was headed. She was determined that I would attend Guardian Angels School at Wynnum, just like my siblings.

First the school had to be convinced, though. Sister Pauline, the head nun, insisted on coming to our home to assess whether I was suitable for the school. She wanted to understand exactly how challenging a student I might be. So Mom organized a visit.

Catherine thought it was very impressive that her school principal was coming to our house.

"Is she going to want to talk to me?" she asked Mom.

Mom paused. "Probably not," she said. "But she may

want to have a look at your bedroom, so you'd better go and clean it up." The visit was a success, and I was outfitted with a new school uniform—gray shorts and a blue shirt. It was time to see if my shiny new pair of artificial legs and my not-so-shiny face would be up to the challenge.

7

Two Apples for David

I wasn't one of those kids who worried about going to school on my first day.

I'd been dispatched to the hospital, admitted overnight and then stayed there for months, brought home for weekend visits, placed in the care of doctors, nurses and specialists, hugged hello and good-bye, and then been picked up perfectly well—sometimes in even better condition—hundreds of times. If nothing else, the hospital had prepared me well for school.

Guardian Angels was a small Catholic elementary school run by an order of monks and an order of nuns. Girls attended until grade seven. Boys stayed only until grade four, then headed to Iona, a combined middle-grade and high school that catered to students from grades five to twelve. One after the other, Michael, Gary, Paula, and Catherine had all managed just fine at Guardian Angels, which was at least some comfort for Mom and Dad.

Mom was worried I might have difficulties getting to the bathrooms, which were up a long flight of stairs from the grade-one classrooms. She petitioned local politicians to provide funds to have a new bathroom block built on the lower level, to no avail. But I was quite capable of using the stairs at home, so there was no reason I couldn't use the stairs at school too.

On my first day of school I was dressed and ready to go half an hour before we had to leave and pestering Mom to get me there as soon as possible. I'd wanted to take the bus to school, like the other kids, but Mom wanted me to spend a few days getting used to school itself before tackling the challenge of the bus. She drove me instead.

I don't remember many details about that day. I remember being lost among a sea of small heads and matching green-and-blue-and-gray uniforms. I remember trees with trunks bursting through the asphalt providing some shade from the sun. I remember older kids playing with tennis balls and skipping ropes. And I remember Mom. I remember her standing there watching me walk away, her face a mix of sadness and pride. It was a scary day for her. Her youngest child was heading off into the wild. She could no longer supervise me all day, every day. There was no knowing what might happen—one of my legs might break, I might fall over, I might be too slow getting from place to place. I might be teased. But I survived that first day unscathed, and returned home happy and excited.

On the second day, Mom walked me to the top of the long, steep steps down to the grade-one classrooms.

"I'll be okay, Mom," I said, letting go of her hand. She looked nervous, but nodded. Two-thirds of the way down, another grade-one boy came up the stairs, heading straight for me. He was walking right alongside the rail. If I wanted to get past, I'd either have to stop and wait for him to pass, or grab the railing on the other side, but there was too much hustle and bustle to try to reach for the other side. I didn't know what to do, so I just kept walking, hoping the other boy would get out of my way. He didn't, and when we reached each other, we both stopped. I looked back for Mom, but could not see her among the wave of kids.

Then I felt a small hand reach out and grab mine. It was

the other boy. We walked down the rest of the stairs hand in hand.

"Hi," I said.

"Hi, I'm David," he said.

"I'm Robert."

David had dark hair and olive skin, and spoke in quiet, clipped tones.

Our classroom was at the bottom of the stairs, and had long wooden racks outside where we left our schoolbags. David took my schoolbag from me, started shoving others' out of the way, and put mine down. Then he took me into the classroom. David did exactly the same thing the next day. I'd made my first friend at school.

At the start of the second week, David went to get my bag.

"Leave it, David," I said. "I can do it myself."

Luckily David was getting something out of the friend-ship too. Mom was sending me to school with sandwiches and an apple. I wasn't always overly keen on eating the apples, and kept giving them to David. It was only fair, I thought, given how much he helped me.

Mom eventually found out. Rather than insist I eat my own apple, she started sending me to school with two apples.

"Now, Robert," she said, "there's one for you *and* one for David, okay?"

I nodded.

"Do you understand, you can both have an apple?"

"Yes, Mom," I said. "Two apples. I understand."

I took the two apples to school. One day when Mom came to pick me up, she saw David and asked if I had given him one of my apples.

"No," David replied with a wide smile. "He gave me *two* apples!"

That first week of school, I did break my leg. I was going up the stairs to meet Mom when one of the metal shafts snapped. David helped me to the car.

Dad phoned the people who had made my legs and they said it could be repaired by anyone who had a spot welder. So Dad took the leg to the local service station to see if they could weld it together.

He walked in and explained what he needed.

"Sorry, mate," the service station owner said. "Too busy."

It was the same story with the second.

At the third service station, the owner took one look at my leg and listened to Dad's explanation.

"This is what I call an urgent job," he said. Then he welded my leg back together, good as new.

After a few weeks, Mom let me start catching the bus to school with Paula and Catherine. The bus stop was about five minutes away—we had to walk up a small hill to the top of our street, around the corner, and then up another small hill.

The first time I only made it up our street and around the corner before stopping.

"I need a rest," I said.

"Why?" Paula asked.

"My legs aren't used to it," I said.

"We haven't got far to go," she said.

I just sat down on the side of the road.

"You've got one minute," Paula said.

After a few more weeks, I adjusted to the journey and could do it more quickly and without having to rest.

If other kids realized exactly how different from them I was when I started school, I didn't notice. Eventually it became obvious when my classmates started asking me questions—the sort of questions Mom and Dad usually answered for me—and I didn't know what to say.

It started to add up pretty quickly. My very first math lesson. Some kids didn't seem to care how I looked, but for every kid who didn't care, there were ten who did.

One gray Monday morning a few weeks after school started, Mom hurried me to get dressed for a hospital appointment.

"Mom, can you put my long pants on?"

"No," Mom said. "I've got shorts here for you. Why would you want long pants on?"

I stayed silent.

"You don't really want to wear long pants, do you?" she asked.

"Yes."

"Why?"

"Some people look at me and say, 'That boy hasn't got any legs. He must have been in an accident,'" I said.

"You don't really care about that, do you?" Mom asked.

"Yes, I do."

"People really aren't trying to be unkind when they say that. If you wear your shorts, they'll be able to see how clever you are and how well you can manage and all the things you can do that they can't do."

I still didn't want to, but I wore shorts.

Medical dramas made it even harder for me to blend in at school. In August 1978, the hospital did a scan that showed a half-inch-wide pocket of infection around some of the bones in my forehead. Infections can eat away at bone, so this was serious. It had the potential to undo all the good work the doctors had done. Dr. Atkinson told Mom and Dad he needed to operate to see what was going on.

Both my parents were on edge, but especially Dad. He now regretted letting me have the big operation, because it seemed to him that afterward I was constantly ill. Before I had been ugly but healthy.

At home, Mom received a bulky envelope from the school that she assumed was schoolwork I'd missed out on. Instead, there were letters from every grade-one student, all reading: "Dear Robert, We love you very much and we hope you will be better soon."

The operation to investigate the infection was very short. After two hours, one of my doctors greeted Mom and Dad at the operating room door. He told them surgeons had cleaned out the infected area. They had removed a few small pieces of wire and silk that had failed to dissolve after my operation the previous February.

I went home at the beginning of December, just in time to finish grade one. Spending months away from school didn't really hinder my education. I'd learned the lessons I was supposed to learn and done well enough at the start of the year to progress to grade two.

After a year of being exposed to other kids, I knew most of them didn't have squashed noses or dents in the sides of their heads where their eyes used to be. Other kids had legs.

You could tickle their feet. I started to realize that each of the kids I regularly saw in the hospital had something different about them. There was the kid in a wheelchair. There was the kid with the strange lump on his neck. But I also started to see them at school too. There was the kid with the harelip. There was the one with flaming red hair and pale white skin. There was the girl who was already taller than all of the boys in the class. There was this one really skinny kid and all the fat ones.

Each one had something different about them. I just had different differences.

8

All Downhill from Here

After I came along there were seven of us in the house in Manly West, a suburb of Brisbane. My two sisters shared one bedroom, while I alternated between sharing a room with my two older brothers and sleeping in a single bed in my parents' room.

Most of the time at home I didn't wear my artificial legs. They were like big, uncomfortable shoes, and every chance I got, I took them off. I could crawl around okay without them on and I was more comfortable. Plus, I had a lot more physical freedom when I had my artificial legs off. I could jump off couches, and jump up and down stairs and crawl around the backyard. I was pretty quick too.

But there were plenty of things my siblings could do that I couldn't, like riding a bike. I'd see my brothers ride their bikes up and down the street, carrying each other on the back—sometimes even on the handlebars in front.

I wanted to ride a bike so much, I thought I'd burst into flames if I didn't.

One day Catherine, Paula, and Gary were playing outside. I asked Gary if I could try riding his bike.

"Sure," he said. "But you'll need your legs on."

When I was wearing my artificial legs they helped me interact better with the big, wide world. I was taller when I had them on, and could walk around like other kids. But that didn't come without a cost. My prosthetics were cumbersome and heavy, and wearing them often made my real legs hot and sore. Imagine wearing a big boot that goes all the way up to your knee, and you'll get a sense of what it's like.

As I was growing, they'd get uncomfortable even faster, because I grew quickly and they didn't fit perfectly for long. I could get around with my legs off—either by crawling or lifting myself up on my arms and swinging the rest of my body underneath me. So almost every chance I could get—especially at home—I took them off.

But riding a bike was worth having my artificial

legs on, so I rushed upstairs and put them on.

"Ready," I said when I came back down.

We were in the front yard. There was the fence and a small avocado tree on one side and the house on the other. About fifteen feet away downhill was the fence to the neighbor's house. In front of it was a lovingly manicured bush grown to chest height. It flowered almost year-round and as far as I could tell, most of the local bee population seemed to live there. I avoided it as much as possible. I'd already been stung by bees a few times and knew how much it hurt.

Gary and Catherine held the bike while Paula helped me climb on.

"What do I do?" I asked.

"Well, you're already facing downhill, so you won't have to pedal much," Paula said.

This was good, because while I could manage to put the foot of my right leg on the pedal, it was impossible to get my left leg sitting comfortably, so it just hung by the side and I tried to keep it out of the way.

"Just steer," Gary said.

"Just steer," Catherine repeated.

"Steer and keep clear of anything, then start pedaling and keep going," Gary said.

Steer and pedal, I thought. Simple.

I gripped the handlebars of the big green bike and leaned forward, head down, built for speed. I imagined gathering speed, pedaling faster and faster, feeling the wind in my hair, going so fast.

"Ready?" Gary said.

I nodded.

And with one mighty shove, I was off.

The first few seconds were sheer terror. I almost fell off as the bike wobbled from one side to another. Then there

was a moment of exhilaration. The bike picked up enough speed to go straight for a little bit. I hadn't fallen off, I hadn't gotten my legs caught in the wheel or the chain, and I hadn't crashed into the side of the house. The wind was in my hair. I was riding a bike!

From behind me, I heard someone shout.

I ignored it at first. The feeling of riding the bike was too much fun.

"Turn!"

"Turn the bike, Robert!"

"Turn!"

Suddenly I was headed straight for the rough branches of the bush on our side of the fence. Turn? They hadn't taught me how to turn, but I turned the handlebars hard to the right and just missed running into the bushes. Or so I thought.

The momentum I'd built going downhill was too strong. While the bike was now traveling parallel to the bushes, I wasn't. I was heading toward them. Or, more precisely, into them. I toppled off the bike and fell straight into the bushes. I immediately started screaming to scare off the bees.

Paula, Catherine, and Gary came racing down the yard to pull me free. I had a few scratches but had avoided any bee stings.

"You didn't turn soon enough," Gary said.

"Not soon enough at all," Paula said.

I scowled at them and started putting myself back together. My bike-riding career had started and finished all in one go.

Another time, Mom and Dad called us all into the living room. This was a rare-enough event, because we were normally scattered—Michael and Gary playing together or getting into fights with their sworn enemies from the house at the top of the street, and Catherine and Paula taking themselves off into their room and doing whatever girls did when they had a secret meeting, which was just talking to each other, as far as I could tell.

We were lined up in the living room from oldest to youngest. Michael, ten years older than me, was tall, almost a mini Dad. He and Gary were similar in looks, with broad faces, big ears, and light-brown hair. They were always exploring, going places I couldn't go and getting there in ways I couldn't—on their bikes, or running. Paula was tall, like Dad, with long dark-brown hair. She talked fast, and lots, and always seemed like the sibling go-between, more patient and willing to play with me than my older brothers. Catherine was closest to me in age, so we played—and fought—together the most. She had red hair and was always being counseled by Mom to stay out of the sun. Like Mom, she was short, but everyone seemed like a giant to me most of the time, especially when I had my artificial legs off.

And I had them off when Mom called us in. I was sitting on the carpet, but everyone else was standing straight. Something was up.

Chocolates had been taken, Mom informed us, from the box on top of the fridge.

"I'm sure whoever took them thought we wouldn't notice," Mom said, walking up and down in front of us.

"I'm sure whoever took them thought, 'Oh, Mom and Dad won't know if one or two are missing.' Unfortunately, there are more than one or two missing. And we did notice that."

She continued walking back and forth in front of us. Dad just stood there, hands behind his back, menacingly tall.

"So," Mom said, "we're going to ask who took the chocolates. We're going to look you in the eye and ask you, and you'd better come clean or there'll be real trouble."

She marched up to one end of the line and looked at Michael. She stared at him for a few seconds.

"Michael, did you take any chocolates?" Mom asked.

I leaned forward slightly so I could get a view of something other than Catherine's knees.

"No," Michael said, looking straight ahead, and then turned toward Gary. Aha, I thought. The culprit. Mom took a step to her right and faced Gary.

"Gary, did you take the chocolates?"

"Nope," Gary said. He turned to look at Paula, next in line.

A look of dread came over Paula's face as Mom stood in front of her. Dad was now moving along the line as well, towering over Mom's shoulder but saying nothing.

"Paula, did you take the chocolates?"

My sister paused for a second and a look of panic flashed briefly across her face.

Surely this meant she was the guilty party, I thought.

But no, Paula regained her composure, turned to look at Catherine first and then back at Mom.

"No, I didn't take any chocolates," Paula said. "It wasn't me."

Mom stared at her a few seconds longer before moving on to Catherine.

The game was up! I knew I hadn't taken the chocolates, and if Michael, Gary, and Paula hadn't taken them either, then it must have been Catherine! I felt bad for Catherine, but I was happy it wasn't me.

"So, Catherine," Mom said, "did you take any chocolates from the box on top of the fridge?"

Catherine looked like she was going to cry. Here it comes, I thought.

Silence for a few more seconds. Her lips trembled slightly. Here it comes!

Then, ever so slowly, like it had been planned this way all along, Catherine turned to look at me. Me!

Wait . . . what? I thought. That wasn't fair. I hadn't done it.

"I didn't take any chocolates," Catherine said, shaking her head. She stared at me the whole time.

I looked to my left and realized there was no one there for me to look at. Not even Sally, our dog.

I started crying before Mom got to me. One by one the others turned to look at me. Dad glared ominously over Mom's shoulder and I tried to say, "It wasn't me. It wasn't me." But everything was lost to my sobbing and I got the blame.

I still don't know who took those chocolates.

9

Names People Play

The first nickname I got at school came not from my classmates but from Catherine.

One day in grade one, Mom arrived to pick us up after school. When I reached the car I was frowning and grumpy. I was carrying my gray jumper rolled up and at arm's length in front of me. Mom was on the case right away. "What happened?" she asked as Catherine and I hopped into the car.

I told her the story. We were in class singing and one of the other boys, who must not have been feeling at all well, vomited on me. I was upset because it had smelled bad and I was worried that Mom would be cranky because my school clothes were messy.

Catherine laughed.

"Ha, ha," she said. "Spewed-on! Spewed-on! Spewed-on!"

I scrunched my face up and almost started to cry.

"Stop it," I shouted at her. "Stop it!" It didn't work.

Mom intervened, but it was too late.

I had been spewed on at school, and now I was "Spewed-on" at home too.

It didn't last long, and luckily, didn't go much further than my family. Plus, our school jumper was pretty ugly to start with.

Have you ever sat on the beach and watched the tide come in? You might not notice the water rising as one wave follows another, but if you wait half an hour, the dry patch you were sitting on is in danger of being overtaken by water. That's what it was like for me at school. The change was gradual, but by the time I was seven, I had started to notice a difference in the way some of my classmates treated me. It's not far from the first gentle wave of genuine interest and curiosity to a crashing tide of teasing and meanness.

The first incident that sticks in my mind was a playground fall. The grounds of our elementary school were quite small. We had plenty of shade under one of the old wooden buildings to eat lunch, but there were no grassy areas for kids to play on during lunch. Each lunchtime, though, a few hundred screaming kids would brave their knees and elbows against the asphalt. Most of the time I'd play in the dirt surrounding the trees that had pushed their way through the hard surface of the playground. I'd play with Matchbox cars or the occasional marble that I'd brought from home.

One day, however, I was running around madly with the other kids. While I couldn't keep up with them for long, I could manage, after a fashion. And what I lacked in speed and maneuverability, I made up for in enthusiasm.

We were playing the schoolyard game of brandy—tag with a tennis ball. It involved throwing the ball as hard as you could at one of the other players, hopefully leaving a lush red mark on some painful but visible part of their body. I was up and had the tennis ball gripped tightly in one hand. A group of other boys were staying just out of range, knowing they could outrun me if they needed to. But that didn't stop me.

I took off with all the speed I could muster, trying to get as close to them as possible before I threw the ball. I ran across the asphalt, which sloped toward the corner of one of the buildings. As I skidded around the corner, something happened. I felt my right leg slip from beneath me. On my way down I managed to throw the ball in the general direction of the other boys. Luckily I fell forward onto my hands, which still hurt, especially on the hot asphalt, but there was no real damage done.

When I looked up to see if my throw had hit its target, the group I was chasing was standing there laughing at me. I probably would have done the same thing, but then one of the boys pointed at me.

"Ha, ha—look at the cripple," he said.

I didn't know exactly what a cripple was, but I was pretty sure, even at that age, that I didn't like it. Some of the others in the group started up too, like noisy kookaburras at sunset.

"Cripple, cripple, cripple!" they shouted.

I picked myself up off the ground and hid from them

for the rest of lunch, but when I got back to class, some of the kids were still calling me cripple.

When I got home I had an afternoon snack and switched on the television. Having attended to these priorities, I turned to Mom.

"Mom, what does 'cripple' mean?"

"It's someone whose legs don't work properly," she said.

"Like me?" I asked.

Mom paused. "Well, yes, sort of like you," she said. "Why? Was someone calling you names at school?"

I didn't realize it at the time, but this was a turning point. It didn't come with a fanfare of angels blowing trumpets and I didn't reflect on it right away. It just happened. I decided to protect Mom from the truth.

Mom asked her question again and I just kind of shrugged and half grinned to hide my embarrassment.

"No. I just heard someone say it the other day," I said. "That's all."

I'm sure my parents could guess every now and then, from my mood or from a stray comment by one of my friends, but I never came out and told them about being teased at school. They had enough to deal with. And more than that—being teased made me feel somehow weak, useless. As if it was my fault. As if I deserved it. As if I hadn't been brave enough to fight it. I couldn't help how I looked or what had happened to me since I was born, but I sure as hell could control how I dealt with people teasing me about it. And my first response was to hide it all away, bury it.

By the time I was seven, the teasing and name-calling did start me thinking more about exactly why I was the way I was. My parents had never told me why—beyond saying I was "born that way"—so on a drive home one day I asked Mom a few questions about it.

"Mom, when I was a baby, did you have a disease or something?" I asked.

"No, I don't think so," Mom said. "Why?"

"Well, then, why are my legs all broken?"

Mom explained that it was because of some medicine she was taking when I was in her tummy, before she knew she was going to have another baby. She'd been feeling sad and the medicine was supposed to make her feel better. Instead, it helped unmake parts of me.

Close to home we passed a gas station that had a small statue out front that looked like a seagull over a fountain. The wishing well of Wynnum.

"Mom, if I put some coins in there, would my special wish come true?"

Mom paused. "What would your special wish be?"

"I'd wish I could buy about sixteen blocks of land and build a kind of Disneyland of my own."

10

Learning to Float

I'd been banned from swimming while I was having all my operations. My doctors said the risk of getting an infection was too high. On vacation at Caloundra every year I was confined to the shallows, sitting on the sand while the water splashed over my lap. I couldn't dive, couldn't let a wave crash over my head, couldn't be taught to swim. Beached at the beach.

By the time I finished grade one, my doctors had relented and told Mom and Dad I could learn, as long as I didn't do any diving into the pool, since that might force water up my nose.

In time, swimming would become a physical freedom

greater than I could ever have imagined. It was one of the few forms of exercise not entirely ruined by my disability. Swimming brought me closer to the physical level of other children. It gave me, if not the chance to excel, at least the opportunity to compete. Most of all, swimming made me free. First, though, I had to learn how.

Mom and Dad took me to Hollands Swim School at Cannon Hill. The instructor did a quick assessment and said I should be able to learn to swim just fine. The next day I came back and had my first half-hour lesson. For a while I had two lessons a week before school and Hollands put me through pretty much all the training they'd do with any kid my age.

While I was learning to use my arms just fine, my legs were more or less useless and couldn't kick. My left leg was so short, it didn't even have a working knee. My right leg was short too and didn't have a foot to help propel me. My arms had to do all the work to pull me along.

The swim school thought I might do better if I could somehow attach a pair of flippers to my legs. Problem was, no feet to attach them to. Mom bought a set of flippers anyway and modified them so they'd fit—and stay on— my legs. She sewed Velcro to the flippers so they could be fastened higher up my legs and strapped with an elastic band around my waist. They were a big help and let me use my lower limbs to provide some extra momentum, but they would only stay on for a minute or so before starting to slide off. Mom tried numerous methods with little success. Then someone had the bright idea of creating a whole-lower-body flipper that I'd pull up over my legs and wear like shorts. I'm lucky they didn't turn me into a mermaid. Or merboy.

The intensive classes were great because they provided one-on-one expertise. I'm sure Dad would have done a fine job teaching me how to swim, just as he had with the other kids, but I was in a hurry to learn, and the extra attention was a big help. Dad and I did end up spending hours swimming at the Manly Baths, the Wynnum Wading Pool, and Caloundra, but most of it was building on the basics I had already learned.

My professional trainer, Kerry, would get cranky at me when I wasn't trying hard enough, and gave me plenty of praise when I did something well. By the time I had been swimming for a month or so, I was ready for my first challenge.

One day at the start of February, Kerry said, "Guess what, Robert?"

"What?"

"I've got a Ronald McDonald watch at home," she said. "When you can swim half the length of the pool, I'll give it to you."

"Wow," I said, and I knew immediately that I must have that watch.

I imagined it to be the best possible watch in the world, and when Kerry brought it to show me at my next lesson, it was just as good as I'd thought it would be. It had a big round face and a shiny black band. And right there in the middle was Ronald himself, red and yellow and smiling and watchy.

By the end of February, it was time to try. I'd been swimming for about eight weeks and was making fair progress. I was on my way to being drown-proofed. Well, drown-proofed if I happened to fall into a pool conveniently only wearing my swimming gear and without my heavy artificial legs on.

I still had that moment of terror when I let go of the side of the pool or was released by someone holding me up in the water. Gripped by a split second of fear, realizing the only thing supporting me was the water, I'd start paddling madly to get somewhere, anywhere that didn't give me this strange feeling of falling-but-not-falling. The paddling would start me moving and I'd still be floating, so I'd calm down enough to realize that if I just kept going, everything would be fine.

Kerry took me out to the middle of the pool and pointed me toward the side. I stayed floating, supported by her hands.

"Ready?" Kerry asked.

"Ready," I said.

Then I was falling through the water. I started to sink—legs first, then down to my waist before I remembered to swim. I started windmilling my arms forward, pulling myself through the water. I was swimming! All on my own! Halfway to the side I remembered to pull my head out of the water, release the breath I'd been holding, and gulp down some more air. As I drew close to the edge, I was getting tired. As much as I wanted the shiny goodness of the Ronald McDonald watch, I felt like I didn't have the energy to make it, and about three feet from the edge of the pool, I stopped.

"Why did you stop there?" Kerry asked.

"I'm pooped," I said. "Can I have a little rest?"

Kerry gave me one of those looks that said, "If you've

got enough energy to stop and say you're pooped while treading water, you've got enough energy to finish."

I kept going.

When I reached the side of the pool, Kerry asked if I wanted to try again.

"I'll stand in the middle of the pool, and if you can reach me, you can have the watch, okay?"

"Okay."

I sucked a few breaths of air in, then put my right leg straight up against the wall and pushed off to get a bit of extra speed. Then I started to swim and in no time flat I'd reached Kerry in the middle of the pool.

"Well done, Robert!" Kerry said.

Mom cheered from the side.

"There's one problem," Kerry said. "I didn't think you'd make it all the way today, so I didn't bring the watch down to the pool with me."

My bottom lip dropped for a second, until she said she'd send someone up to the house to get it. By the time I was out of the pool and had dried myself, the watch was there, bright and new and as Ronald McDonaldish as could be. Mom made me get dressed before I could put it on. I waved it around and held it in front of her face.

"This is a real good watch, isn't it?"

Mom nodded.

She let me wear it in the car to school. When I got there I rushed ahead to show my teacher.

"Sister, Sister. Look what I got."

She half smiled and nodded. "You are a spoiled boy, aren't you?"

"Robert, tell Sister why you got the watch," Mom said.

I told Sister Marie Patrice about the swimming lesson

and how I'd made it halfway across the pool without any-one helping at all and that I'd been given the watch as a reward.

"Well, Robert, I think you deserve it, then."

Mom said good-bye and made me give her back the watch so I didn't lose it at school. That was kind of sad, but at least I could put it on as soon as I got home and show Dad and my brothers and sisters and tell the whole story again and again.

I'd learned how to swim well enough to make it about fifteen feet on my own. Now all I had to do was stop getting quarter past the hour and quarter to the hour confused and learn how to tell time properly.

The Guardian Angels kids had been going to Iona regularly to swim in the pool there. Not me. Disabled by land, disabled by sea. After my success at Hollands, I asked Mom if I could start swimming with the rest of my classmates.

"Please, Mom," I said.

Mom talked to the teachers one morning when she dropped me off. She told them about my lessons and said Dad would come down whenever he could. The teachers told Mom they were happy for me to join the others, and she came to find me in the playground to give me the good news.

When she told me I hollered and ran to tell David. It was a small victory in the battle to be less different from everyone else.

11

Friends and Enemies

The operations the doctors had done on my face over the years started to pay off. I made new friends at school and at home. Some kids were quick to see how different I was, but many others seemed not to notice, or at least not to care. I wasn't the most popular kid in school. I didn't have people rushing to spend every possible second with me at lunch. But I wasn't totally shunned and ignored either.

David and I were still friends, but I made a bunch of new ones too. Chief among my new school friends were Robert Firmin and Robert Webb. For a while we became the three Roberts—referred to as Robert H, Robert F, and Robert W. I had an easy connection with Robert F. Before a growth spurt, he had been of average height and a bit awkward. We both loved books and stories about stars and distant planets and spaceships. At Guardian Angels we'd started hanging out, talking about space and astronomy. Robert W was fun to hang around with too, but I think the main reason I wanted to be friends with him was because his name was Robert. After all, it wouldn't have been the three Roberts if there were only two of us.

There were friends at home as well. Manly West was still a young suburb when I was growing up—especially compared to nearby Wynnum. There were a few kids my age living right near our house. They were all girls, but that didn't matter to me. There was Cassandra, who lived next door, and down the road were Belinda and Evelyn. Evelyn's family didn't have a lot of money, and sometimes Mom would send us down to her house with tins of food. Often it was canned beets, which suited me just fine, as I thought they were horrid and we always had so much of them.

To me, Cassandra was the most important. The others would come and go, but Cassandra and I were constants. She was the only child of a couple living next door, so she was always happy to get out of the house and play. She was even happier to come and join in the loud chaos of a large family like ours. Cassandra and I would spend whole afternoons chasing each other around one backyard, then over the fence into the other. We'd bounce on her trampoline for hours on end. She would run up and down the sidewalk and I'd go up and down the road on a skateboard, artificial legs off, propelling myself forward with my arms. We'd play with Legos—she always had more Legos than me, but that was okay because I had a much higher proportion of space Legos, and if there was one thing you needed to build spaceships, it was space Legos.

We'd grab the old transistor radio her parents had given her, go outside at night, raise the antenna, and point it at the stars. Right at the bottom of the AM dial, just when you almost couldn't turn it any further, we'd pick up strange signals, rhythmic electric pulses that could only be one thing: UFOs.

Cassandra would sometimes turn up at our back door and politely ask Mom or Dad if I was home and would like to play. For my part, I'd go down to the fence between our two houses and yell, "Cassandra!" as loud as I could, a human megaphone.

Because Dad was a shift worker and would often start work early the next day, we'd have dinner at 5:30 or 6 p.m.

and listen to the news. From 6 p.m. to 7 p.m. was TV-viewing time for Mom and Dad. Without fail, the television would be switched to some news or current-affairs program. Much to my horror, this meant missing shows like *The Goodies* and especially *Doctor Who*. I'd go over to Cassandra's house right after dinner so I could watch *Doctor Who*.

We'd listen, sometimes scared, for any familiar-but-strange alien signals. When the show finished I'd head home so I could have a shower and get ready for bed.

She was my best friend for a long time, even when I

became a typical boy and was afraid to admit it.

Together, Cassandra, Evelyn, Belinda, and I had plenty of adventures. A few years in a row we sold grapefruit on the corner. They were picked from a tree in Cassandra's yard. We made signs and moved a table onto the sidewalk. Given all our efforts—tree-climbing, grapefruit-picking, sign design, and drawing—we priced the grapefruit at fifty cents each. I decided the best form of advertising was to stand on the corner of our street and yell at the top of my voice, "Grapefruits for sale!"

I think in the first year we sold a grand total of one grapefruit. Next grapefruit season we were right back at it, though—picking, making signs, and selling. Again, my chief duty was to stand on the corner and yell at the top of my voice, "Grapefruits! Grapefruits for sale! Get your grapefruits!" The first day we had no luck, selling a total of zero grapefruits. We went home dejected.

Next morning we assembled to give it another go. It didn't look like we were going to make our fortunes in grapefruit sales that year either. Then someone walked up and asked how many grapefruits we had. Cassandra said we had about a dozen, in various stages of ripeness. The customer asked if she could buy all of them for ten dollars. Absolutely, we said, after conferring with each other for exactly three seconds. A whole ten dollars! That was a fortune to us. The neighbor handed over the money and we handed over the grapefruits, happier and richer than we had ever been in our little lives.

Things changed when we told Cassandra's parents. We were excited and asked if they could take the ten dollars and split it four ways for us. Concerned that the neighbor had spent so much on our enterprise, they decided we should go and give half of it back. Suddenly our fortune was only half a fortune, but give it back we did. I think they must have thought the poor lady had only bought all the grapefruits to shut me up.

The three girls were a little younger than me, and they seemed to adjust to me pretty quickly. Young kids are naturally very accepting of new and different things. The kid with a squishy nose and strange legs isn't that surprising when you're three years old and you hear stories about talking bears sitting at a table eating porridge. It's only as kids get older that they start to know what's normal and what's not.

We used to congregate on sidewalks, in backyards, and at a nearby park to play on the swings and scheme and scamper along the local creek, building bridges and trying to catch the small fish in the little stream. The girls would do cartwheels and I'd practice handstands without my prosthetics on. One day when I took my legs off, Evelyn pointed at them.

"Oh! What happened to your feet?"

"Nothing," I said.

"Who chopped them off?" Evelyn asked.

"No one," I said.

"Did you chop them off?" Still with the questions.

"No."

"Did the doctors chop them off?"

"No."

"Were you born like that?"

"Yes."

And we kept on playing.

Other questions weren't always quite so easy to answer. Sometimes I'd get asked, "How did you lose your legs?" As if I'd left them on the bus and they were waiting to be reclaimed from the lost and found.

Outright sympathy could be just as frustrating. Sometimes passersby would tilt their head and deliver an undeserved smile. "Look at the kid limping along the sidewalk," the smile would say. "Isn't he wonderful/inspirational/amazing."

There were some things I just couldn't avoid when it came to my disability.

The first was knowing I'd need to work smart during my life because I wasn't going to be able to work hard physically.

When I came home from school with a bad test score, Mom would look at me sternly and Dad would say what he always said. At various times Dad had been a meat worker, a cane cutter, a forklift driver, and a lawn-mower man. He knew I had a different path.

"Robert," Dad would say, "you're not going to be digging ditches for a living. You've got to try harder."

The second was that I seemed to have more of a sense than most kids about the physical space surrounding me. The way I experienced the physical world was always changing. If you have two artificial legs, sometimes you're short and sometimes you're tall. Sometimes you experience the world on all fours, jumping from place to place. Other times, you have your legs on and operate the way the world intended, except when you stumble or your legs start aching fifteen minutes after you've put them on.

The third thing was that there weren't a lot of people like me I could look up to. Men are meant to be strong. We are supposed to be powerful. Dad and Michael and Gary were tall and broad-shouldered. Most of the men I saw on TV were built well and active too. There were no disabled role models for a young boy trying to work out what sort of man he could become.

Those issues didn't have simple answers. I'd have to work out how to make my own way in the world.

12

We All Fall Down

It was July 1979 and the American space agency, NASA, had a problem.

The first space station it had launched was about to fall to Earth. Skylab, a 77-ton, 26-meter-long chunk of metal, had orbited Earth for six years. Scientists onboard had successfully conducted hundreds of experiments and undertaken thousands of observations. About one hundred and seventy photographs of the sun and the Earth were taken. Astronauts did forty-two hours of spacewalks.

But by the mid-1970s, Skylab was in trouble. If its orbit wasn't corrected, it was going to crash to Earth. For a while NASA had planned to use the new space shuttles it was building to repair Skylab and boost its orbit, but a delay meant they weren't ready in time. Skylab was on its own. And it was falling down.

There was tremendous media interest about Skylab falling to Earth, certainly enough to capture the attention of a boy who was about to turn seven and had already started dreaming about the stars. It was expected to crash somewhere in the southern hemisphere. Surely that meant there was every chance it could crash into Australia, I thought.

NASA couldn't be sure, but I was. It was going to hit us.

Luckily, David and I had a plan.

The parts of Skylab that fell to Earth would—conveniently—fall on the bathroom block at Guardian Angels. The entire school would—conveniently—be inside the bathroom block at the time. I'm guessing at this stage that it was the boys' bathroom, but we—conveniently—skipped over some of those details. Anyway, Skylab would crash into the school, we'd all be in the bathroom and the crash would—conveniently—collapse the entrance and we would be trapped. If everything went to plan, it would be a convenient convenience.

With everyone at school trapped inside, there would be no one to rescue us, and we'd need to find our own way out.

David and I worked out that I would give him one of my artificial legs, which he would use as a battering ram. He could then smash the debris and rubble out of the way and free us all. We were so prepared, we even had detailed engineering diagrams—in crayon—of what the rescue would look like.

But that wasn't the way things went down.

Instead of landing on Brisbane, Skylab broke up, with some parts falling into the Indian Ocean off Western Australia. Other major parts rained down hundreds of miles east of Perth. Almost two thousand five hundred miles away in Brisbane, my chance to be a school hero had crashed and burned as well.

Flaming chunks of metal crashing from the sky weren't the only things falling down in the late 1970s.

Like most schools, Guardian Angels had an annual field day. The fact that I had no legs did not excuse me from participating. Apparently, if God did not want me to race, he would not have given me artificial legs.

For sports day we all trekked to Iona, where Michael and Gary both went, and where I would presumably end up too. Iona had several sports fields of its own—more than enough room for the few hundred students from our small elementary school.

There were events like tunnel ball and tug of war, but the real highlight was the sprints. I was entered in the hundred-meter sprint along with all the other kids. It was as compulsory as soggy tomato sandwiches at snack time. Catherine was still at Guardian Angels, so she came along to race as well, and Mom and Dad were both there to see us run.

Dad was unsure about me competing. It wasn't that he didn't want me to run—quite the opposite. He was just concerned about me being made into a spectacle.

But Mom was insistent.

"I know Robert can't win," she told Dad at the time. "But he can get in there and try."

She didn't want to tell me that I wouldn't be able to keep up and had no chance of winning. She was worried that I'd sit on my backside and give up, that I'd stop trying.

Race day came and I got all dressed up and ready to run. Mom had bought me a new white sports T-shirt, green shorts, one sneaker and one long white sock. The shoe and sock would go on my right leg, which had an actual artificial foot. My left foot was still just a horse's hoof of solid metal.

We sat on the dusty hill next to Iona's main oval and watched as small, uncoordinated kids ran race after race. Mixed among them were a few athletes who stood out with their speed and grace.

Then it was my turn, and I lined up with the other kids. Mom and Dad stood on the sidelines.

"I still don't like it," Dad said.

"Well, Vince," Mom said, "if you feel like walking over there and taking him out of the race, you can, but I'm not about to."

It was too late anyway. I was on the starting line—skinny kids on either side of me with big eyes, bad haircuts, and white T-shirts of their own—and happy to give it a go. I bent down and leaned forward, pushing my arms out in front of me like I was going to somehow box my way into the race. I wasn't thinking about running a record time or qualifying for the Olympics or being a spectacle. I just wanted to run. And win.

"On your marks," the starter shouted. "Get ready—" *Bang!*

For at least four strides I kept up with the other kids.

I was taking what seemed like giant steps with my right

leg. I had no working left knee—real or artificial—and most of the leg consisted of just two pieces of straight metal. As I ran I had to swing that leg in a semicircle away from my body. Normally I was fairly disciplined about keeping it close to my body to try to disguise my limp. It was still obvious that it wasn't a real leg, but I did my best. All of that went out the window as soon as I started to run. I swung my left leg wildly to my side, almost knocking over a kid in the next lane.

About thirty feet into the race, I was already way behind the others, but I just kept powering on. I could still catch them. When I realized I was probably going to be last, I started swinging my arms faster—that's what they did on television—and tried to pump my legs faster. That only made me swing my left leg wider and wilder. About a third of the way into the race I was going so fast—for me—that I started to trip.

I felt myself tumbling forward and tried to stop but it was no use. Down I went. I fell forward, which I was used to. The grass on the oval at Iona was soft and I wasn't really hurt. I picked myself up and saw that the other kids were well over halfway done but not yet finished. Still time to catch them, I thought. I powered on, arms and legs swinging, puffing away. By the time I reached the halfway point, the other kids were crossing the finishing line.

Now I was racing myself, really. Racing on my own but not alone. Parents and teachers nearby started cheering me on, and I finished the race feeling like a winner. The timekeeper at the finish line later said he had to ask the other kids in the race who'd won because everyone was watching me instead.

Mom asked me if I minded not winning.

"No, of course not," I said.

Later, Catherine ran her race and managed to come in last as well.

I turned to Mom and said, "Look, Catherine came in further last than I did."

Falling over and finishing last in a running race and bashing my way out of buildings after space stations crashed on them were all well and good. But eventually I realized I could use my disability to make people laugh.

One afternoon, Mom came to pick me up from school early for an appointment. She came to our classroom, but my teacher, Sister Marie Patrice, was off talking to another teacher in a different room. Everyone in the class had their heads down, but someone saw Mom waiting at the door. The kids started shouting out, "Hello, Mrs. Hoge!" and I jumped up.

I'd got into the habit of loosening the long laces that held the leather socket tight to my left stump when I sat down. As I stood up, my artificial leg started to rattle loose. It was a shock at first, but then I started shaking my left stump wildly until my artificial leg fell off entirely. I was holding myself up with my hands on nearby desks and hopping on one leg.

"Hi, Mom!" I shouted.

David jumped up and started hopping around too, almost tripping on my leg, which was now on the floor. Others were about to join in when Mom saw Sister Marie Patrice walking back.

"Quick, hurry, Sister," she called out.

Ratted out by my own mother!

I sat down and quickly grabbed my leg from the floor as the fearsome nun stood at the door next to my mother and gave us a strange look.

"Robert and David, come here, please," she said.

I'd only half finished putting my leg on and hadn't tightened up the laces, but I was so frightened, I started walking to the door.

David got to the teacher first and she gave him a whack on the bottom.

"In the future, behave," she said.

"Yes, Sister," David said, and went and sat back down at his desk.

Then it was my turn. She gave me a harmless whack on the bum, but for some reason I overbalanced and fell forward. My left leg, still not properly secured, fell off. It toppled in one direction and I toppled in the other.

Sister Marie Patrice just got redder and redder. She was probably the maddest I had ever seen her.

A hush came over the whole class. A few kids at the back stood up so they could see. They burst out laughing until they got one of Sister Marie Patrice's looks.

"Put that leg on," she said, "and get up." Then she turned to Mom, looking horrified. "This has never happened in my classroom before," she said.

Mom, who had done a very good job of keeping her composure the whole time, finally burst out laughing.

I was starting to realize that while kids laughing at you

could be very hurtful, kids laughing at something you'd done was a different thing entirely.

That wasn't the only time I caused grief for poor Sister Marie Patrice. Because our school was so close to the water, we'd regularly walk the block down to the shore for a quick excursion. Sometimes it was to look at the islands dappled across the horizon; other times to talk about the jetty and how boats might have used it in days gone by. I'm sure it was occasionally just an excuse to get us kids out of the classroom and have us run around on the grass.

Moreton Bay is bordered on the north by Redcliffe and on the south by Wellington Point, with Wynnum in the middle. It is protected by Moreton Island and North Stradbroke Island, which means calm waters and no surf. When the tide went out, it went almost three hundred feet—about three-quarters of the way along the jetty at Wynnum. It left behind a vast expanse of mud, seaweed, shells, and the occasional, very unlucky jellyfish.

One day, Sister Marie Patrice took the class down to the foreshore. The tide was out and soon enough a few of us had scattered and found our way onto the mudflats. The other kids took their shoes off before they squelched around in the mud, but I figured with my artificial legs, everything would be just fine.

Unfortunately I got a bit too adventurous. After stepping out from the shore, I saw some interesting rocks that I wanted to investigate. This was a wet, smelly mistake. I ventured farther from the shore, but my left leg sank deep into the mud, well beyond where my ankle would have been. Any normal kid would have used his or her knee to pull the leg up and out of the mud, but I had no left knee. Instead, I started working my leg back and forward, trying to create enough room to swing it out. That didn't work. It just made the leg sink further.

As I tried to work my left leg free, I put all my weight on my right leg, until it started to sink as well. I flailed my arms about, consumed by images of quicksand from old Tarzan movies and episodes of *Gilligan's Island*. I looked for a vine I could grab on to, but there were none nearby.

I paused for a moment to think and noticed that I stopped sinking when I didn't move. I figured I could just stand there for a while and see what happened, though the tide would come in eventually, I supposed. The other kids were doing their own thing, oblivious to me. I decided I'd give it one more go. A big effort. Surely that would work. I took a deep breath and pushed forward, trying as hard as I could to drag my left leg up and out of the mud. For a second it felt like it was working, but then I lurched too far. I was used to falling over—well practiced at it, in fact. I'd feel myself falling, shove my hands forward and lock my elbows and shoulders as tightly as I could, and fall. Better to end up with sore palms than to face-plant.

But it was not the right strategy this time.

I shoved my hands out in front of me, locked my elbows and shoulders, and slowly toppled over. I was expecting the usual jarring thud, but my hands didn't stop when they hit the mud. Instead, they kept going, into the slimy mire— past my wrists, past my forearms, stopping just as the mud reached my elbows. I now had all four limbs stuck in the mud. I let out a slight squeal of panic.

Behind me, I heard a loud gasp. Sister Marie Patrice must have spotted me. There was no mistaking the sound of a nun who was equal parts concerned, annoyed, and frustrated that she'd have to wade into the mud herself to save one of her more stupid students.

Suddenly the mud didn't seem so bad.

By then the other kids had seen me as well, and those

who'd disobeyed the instruction not to go out too far started making their way back to safety.

Sister Marie Patrice lifted up the long skirt of her habit and for the first time in my life I saw her ankles. Quickly those lily-white ankles became covered in mud. As she got close, I thought I was going to cop a whack on the bum, but when she reached me Sister Marie Patrice just grabbed my arms and tried to pull me out. No luck.

Then she grabbed my left leg and, with what I assumed was Jesus-powered strength, slowly dragged it up out of the mud. Then she kind of lifted me up and over. My hands came out first, then my right leg with a vacuum plop as the mud rushed to fill the newly vacated space. It took us a while and I was really tired from all the exertion, but eventually we made our way back to solid ground.

I had mud on my shoe, on my sock, on my artificial legs, inside my artificial legs, on my gray shorts, on my shirt, under my fingernails and halfway up my arms.

"Now, Robert, don't you go back out there, understand?"

I nodded. "Yes, Sister."

I sat on the retaining wall and watched her walk away. She looked back at me a few times, but I just stared innocently out at St. Helena Island, thinking about the people who'd been so bad they had to be sent away from a penal colony to a special prison on an island all its own. Finally she was far enough away, paying attention to other kids.

I could have a bit of a look around, I thought. It would be okay if I didn't go too far.

I ventured back out onto the mudflats. And got stuck. Again.

13

Games Not Played

One afternoon I returned from school extremely excited.

"Mom, Mom, I've got something to show you!" I yelled. "Can I, Mommy? Can I?"

"How about you tell me what it is you want?"

I rummaged in my schoolbag, pushing aside books and pencils and half-squished bananas I hadn't gotten around to eating, and pulled out a sheet of paper. It was a permission slip for parents to sign, allowing their boys to play school sports.

"Can I? Can I? Can I play?"

"Stop!" Mom said. "I'm trying to read this properly."

She read it once, then turned it over, but there was nothing on the back. She read it again, taking it slow. Then a third time.

"Well, I'd like to have a think about it and talk to Dad," she said. "Is that okay?"

Everyone else in the family was involved in sports in one way or another. Even Mom, who didn't really play anything much, had started managing the tennis team Catherine played on.

The sport I wanted to play was called rugby league.

Rugby league is a lot like American football, but with no helmets and no pads. And fewer cheerleaders. Two teams of thirteen players line up against each other on a grassy, rectangular field. Each team tries to carry the ball downfield and score a try, like a touchdown. Teams had six tackles, or downs, to score before the opposing team took possession of the ball and tried to score.

It was a simple game, and where I lived, it was the most popular sport to play and to watch.

Even for young kids, though, it was a tough contact sport. You ran at a bunch of kids standing in front of you trying to block your way and either somehow managed to break through, or a bunch of them would fall on you when you didn't. It was a mess of arms and legs going all over the place. One way or another, you'd come into violent contact with some other kid.

Mom and Dad were under instructions from my doctors to avoid knocks to my head. Surgeons didn't want a forearm or a foot undoing all their good work. Neither did my parents.

Just as bad was the chance another player could cop a whack from one of my artificial legs. Both were much harder than a real leg and could cause some serious harm.

There was no way Mom and Dad could let me play.

Mom went to school to see Mr. French, who was in charge of organizing the teams for our school. She explained to him the reasons I couldn't play and asked if there was some way I could be involved on the sidelines. They came up with a plan for me to be a ball boy on the side of the field, kicking the ball back in when it came out of bounds, and helping players set up the ball for place kicks.

"Do you mind if you only play on the sidelines, Robert?" Mom asked when she arrived home.

"I don't mind what I do or where I am, as long as I'm playing and as long as I'm there."

She and Dad both made a show of signing the permission slip, but I'm not really sure it ever made its way to school.

We won that first game. I even got to go on the field a few times. It felt good, but deep down I knew I wasn't part of the team.

A year later, I came home from school one day and called to Mom from my bedroom while I was getting changed, asking her if I could play Saturday morning rugby league. No reply. I guessed she hadn't heard me.

Later, I went to my schoolbag and retrieved the slip of paper with all the information on it. I put it on the table in front of her.

"Give me a straight answer, yes or no," I said.

"Would you be very disappointed if I said no?" Mom asked.

I started to cry.

Once again, Mom explained that it was a tough contact sport. I was likely to be hurt if an elbow or a foot hit me in the face, and other players were likely to be hurt if a clump of metal from one of my legs hit their head.

I just kept crying.

We watched rugby league every Sunday night on television. Sometimes I even got to go with Dad and watch games at the stadium. The players were some of my biggest heroes.

"Maybe you could play tennis," Mom suggested.

"I don't want to play tennis!" I shouted at her.

Mom almost lost her temper then, but she took a long breath and closed her eyes for a moment before responding.

"I'll talk to Dad about it when he gets home from work."

I stormed off, sulking.

Next morning, I grabbed the sheet of paper and excitedly plonked it in front of Dad at the breakfast table.

"Can I play, Dad?"

"No, Robert. You can't play," he said.

I started crying again. "Why not?"

"It's too dangerous," Mom said. "If you play a sport like that, you'll just end up hurting yourself or someone else."

I crossed my arms, like I'd seen people do on television when they were cranky but determined.

Dad tried to cheer me up. "These kids kick each other in the shins and they put their fingers up each other's nose when no one is looking," he said.

I didn't laugh.

"Are you sure you don't want to play tennis?" Mom asked.

"Yes."

"Well, go have your bath and get ready for school, then," she said.

"I'm not going to school," I said.

Mom shrugged. "Suit yourself."

Dad glowered at me and pointed toward the bathroom, and I went.

When I came home from school, Mom again talked to me about tennis. I still wasn't very keen, but after a while Mom sent me into her bedroom to retrieve a package, all wrapped up, that she'd left on the bed.

"It's a tennis racket!" It was just like the one Catherine had.

I was excited to have my own tennis racket at first, but I didn't really pursue the sport or make the most of the training Mom and Dad offered. I wanted to be part of a team, win, lose, or draw—but mostly win.

We'd go around in circles every few months. I'd argue that I should be allowed to play some sport and my parents would say no. Summer was cricket season but that would involve having a hard, heavy ball aimed at my body at significant speed. It was another no.

I loved swimming too, but it wasn't the kind of team

sport I wanted to play and I wasn't fast enough to be competitive. Running was the same as swimming, with the added benefit that I fell over all the time. One by one, all the sports were eliminated.

In elementary school, the closest I got to any organized competition was Friday-afternoon sports. Most of the other kids would go off to play competitions against nearby schools, but there'd be a bunch of us left behind—the injured, the uncommitted, the uncoordinated, the ones who couldn't catch. The crippled.

I would have happily spent my time in the library. Alas, this gaggle of uncoordinated misfits was rounded up each week and made to play some sort of sport against each other. We'd get into our sports gear and head down to one of the ovals not being used for a real sport. We'd be told what "sport" we were going to play for the afternoon. Often it was softball, but sometimes it was a made-up sport designed to at least keep us active for the last hour and a bit of the school week.

The teacher would choose two captains. The captains would then look the rest of us over, using their obvious years of sporting experience, training, coaching, and performing at the highest levels of athletic competition. And they'd slowly put us poor suckers out of our misery.

It would start like this. Whichever captain had first pick would select the super-competitive skinny kid who didn't play an organized sport because his parents were worried he'd break something. It was rare but not unknown to have some kids with actual athletic talent with us there on those Friday afternoons. Then the captains would make their way through the kids who had some skills but weren't as well-rounded: the kid who could catch but couldn't bat; the kid who could bat but couldn't run.

The first few times, I waited with excitement for my name to be called. I couldn't run fast, but the teacher always allowed someone else to run for me if we were playing something like softball. I figured my chances of getting picked were as good as those of anyone else.

My hopes were soon dashed, though. It became very obvious very quickly that even on a team of nobodies with no sporting talent and often even less enthusiasm, no one was keen to pick me.

The captains would keep going until there were only three or four students left. This is where things would get really interesting. The two captains would look over and see that it was a choice between the crippled kid, the kid who could not catch a ball even if it was dropped gently into his cupped hands from inches above, the kid who had a cast taken off their broken ankle only last week, and the kid who just couldn't get the rules of any game, no matter how often you tried to explain them.

The captains would be down to their second-to-last choice. They'd look us over, look at each other, sometimes look at the teacher, and invariably they'd call out: "Robert."

I'd hear my name and I'd limp on over to my team-mates, occasionally issuing a high five and talking about how we were going to crush our opponents. But in my heart I'd know there was no honor in being chosen second to last.

Every now and then I'd get my hopes up, thinking maybe I'd be recognized for my brilliant tactical or motivational skills and would be chosen first for a change. Other times I would have been happier to be picked last—it would have been honest, at least. But no. Second to last had become the new last.

When you're a young boy who loves sports, there's hardly anything worse than being picked second to last for a sporting team, knowing the captain probably would have picked you last but didn't because he either felt sorry for you or was worried he'd get a disapproving look from the teacher.

It seemed like there was no sport for me to play.

People sometimes assumed I had been play-

ing a sport when I was "injured," which seemed unfair—even cruel—when I wanted to play so badly and wasn't able to.

When I was twelve, I once went into an elevator by myself. Two middle-aged ladies got in after me. One of them looked me up and down, then stared at my face long enough to make me look away.

"Terrible how they let kids so young play rough sports these days," she said to her friend. "Look at the damage it does."

The other woman turned and stared at me too. "Yes, yes it is," she said.

Some of the best talks I have ever had started with someone asking, "This might seem rude, but can I ask about your face/nose/scars/bumps?" Wherever those conversations ended up, they started as honest exchanges. Acknowledging someone's differences can be about saying you're not scared to talk to someone about the things that make them who they are.

Those few moments in the elevator were not one of those times and I stayed silent until we reached the ground floor.

I should have cringed or felt embarrassed or angry at those two women, but at the time I just wanted to laugh. Lady, if only you knew how much I wished I was this ugly because I was allowed to play sports!

14

Things Written Down

Things in class were almost as dire as they were on the sporting field.

I made it to grade three, where I had my first male teacher, Mr. French. He was tall with a booming voice and a bushy beard. The nuns I'd had in grades one and two were mysterious, unknowable, but Mr. French was a civilian.

We spent long days tackling spelling and multiplication and grammar. But we seemed to spend most of our time on handwriting. We were expected to master "running writing," or cursive. My attempts were so shaky, so misshapen, so ugly, it looked like I'd interpreted running writing to mean writing done while running in a race.

"Not good enough, Robert. You've got to try harder," Mr. French said again and again. "Don't hurry so much. Slow down and think about what you're doing with your pen."

Finally, it was time for a test. Not a spelling test or a vocabulary test. A handwriting test. Mr. French would read out a sentence and we had to write it down as neatly as we could. I slowed down and did okay for the first three or four letters. But I quickly fell behind as Mr. French read the next sentence and I had to rush to catch up. This meant messy letters again. After a few painful sentences, we finished. My paper might as well have been covered in the etchings of an alien language, written left-handed while standing on my head. In a pool. My test came back with a single checkmark on the entire page and lots of very precise, neat X-marks. One out of ten.

Mr. French called me and two other kids to the front of the class. He told us there was no reason for handwriting that messy and we clearly hadn't been practicing. I started going red. It was the first time I'd been called out in front of the class for bad schoolwork.

Then he said four words that scarred me for life. "Hold out your hands." Schools at the time still punished students by whacking their hands or bottoms with straps or a long, thin piece of wood called a cane. We were going to get the cane! I'd been in trouble at school before, but most of the time, that just meant a whack on the bottom from one of the nuns.

After I heard the initial whack, I wished I'd been first in line. I closed my eyes and started to slowly curl my fingers.

"Hand flat, Robert," Mr. French said as he approached me.

He brought the cane down on my hand and I thought it was going to split in two. It left a cranky red mark across my hand. My writing hand. I closed my eyes again and tried not to cry.

Right then and there I decided that what my words meant and said were more important than how they looked. I decided I'd always choose writing faster over writing neat. I'd sacrifice legibility on the altar of speed. Looks didn't matter so much.

Grade four was worlds better.

I had one of the best teachers of all my school years, Gary Bolton. He was young and energetic. He played the guitar and taught us how to make tacos. He showed us batik, letting us paint wax patterns on cloth and T-shirts and spill dye everywhere. And he read us passages from *The Lord of the Rings*, in which the two tiny hobbits, Frodo and Sam, are taken by the evil Gollum into the lair of the giant spider, Shelob. Gollum leads them there as a ruse, so Shelob can sting them and he can regain the ring.

I'd be one of the kids clamoring for "more, more please, sir" when Mr. Bolton would eventually sigh and say it was enough for that day. I told him how exciting it was to be hearing a story from such a big book.

"You know what, Robert?" he said. "Maybe you could write one of your own someday."

I'd never really thought about that before.

Life outside of the classroom was changing for me too.

I was getting better at dealing with other kids. If someone started teasing me, I did my best to ignore it. I was also starting to understand that I could try to ignore or shake off the way I felt when people called me names. At home, I was learning how to deal with my four older siblings, learning how to argue—even while losing 82 percent of the arguments I had with them and almost all of the arguments I got into with my parents. I was starting to understand what was easy and comfortable and what was more challenging. I was starting to conquer my disability and grasp my place in the small world I inhabited.

Then I met my first true love.

Her name was Michelle. She was new to the school. Michelle and her older sister were just starting at Guardian Angels that year. She had deep brown eyes and hair three shades from red. She was in Mr. Bolton's class with me, enjoying math and English and batik and eating tacos along with everyone else. She seemed distant but in a warm way that felt like she just really hadn't got to know many people yet.

I decided she simply had to be my girlfriend.

I didn't know much about girls, but I knew I couldn't just go up to her and say something. I wondered for a little while about the best way to communicate my deep-felt passion and decided to commit it to paper. I grabbed a pencil and ripped a sheet of paper from my exercise book. The page came out with a ragged tear and the pencil turned out to be a green one, but that would have to do. In my head, what I wrote read like the most exquisite poem ever committed to paper by a ten-year-old. It was smart and beautiful—poetry from a midget Shakespeare. Mr. Bolton had said maybe I could write a book someday, so surely this would be easy.

The next challenge was to deliver the poem to Michelle. I thought about leaving it for her in class, but I had the sense that it might end up getting me in trouble. My best bet would be to deliver the note at lunchtime. Find Michelle, give her the note, and wait for endless love. Easy. The problem was that the girls and boys played in different parts of the playground. There was the occasional border skirmish, but crossings from one side to the other were rare.

I stood near the border of the girls' area, waiting, trying to spot Michelle. Robert F came and joined me and asked what I was doing.

"I'm looking for Michelle," I said. "To give a message to her."

"Can't see her," Robert F said.

"Nope."

A few other boys came to join us and when I explained what I was doing one of them shouted out, "Hey, girls. Come here for a second, would you? Hey, girls!"

It was loud enough to attract attention and two girls wandered over.

"Robert wants to get this message to Michelle. Can you find her and give it to her?"

One of the girls nodded. She held out her hand and I gave her the note containing what felt like the two most important sentences I'd ever write. The girl then moved a few steps away and said, "We'll give it to Michelle. But we need to read it first."

"No!" I yelled, horrified.

The girl smiled and slowly unfolded the note.

"You want Michelle to be your girlfriend," she said. "You!"

The other girl laughed too and a couple of the boys behind me sniggered. Then came the reminders.

"You've got a funny nose," one of the girls said.

"And no legs," one of the boys behind me said.

"Give it back," I said.

"No, we'll make sure we get it to Michelle."

The school bell called us back to class and the girl turned and ran. I tried to chase her but she was faster than me. The note was either on its way to Michelle or to someone else entirely. I didn't have any idea what to do, but I had to get back to class. I spent the rest of the day worried that the message had been delivered to Michelle and equally worried that it hadn't. I didn't look at her once the whole afternoon.

After endless nervous hours, school was over for the day. I was packed up, schoolbag over my shoulder and ready to go faster than anyone. Or so I thought. Michelle was faster. Before I could move, she was there standing in front of my desk.

"Hi, Robert," she said, and smiled.

"Hi, Michelle," I said.

Now would be a good time to magically grow legs so I could run away, I thought.

"I got your note," she said.

"Oh." I could tell by the look in her eyes that it was not going to be good news.

Michelle declined my offer of boyfriendship.

"It's just, you're a boy," she said.

I shrugged and escaped as fast as I could without saying a word. My love letter had only two sentences and later I figured out I had spelled her name wrong. I didn't even think to sign my name to it. Not my most successful piece of writing ever. I'd done it in a hurry too, so it wasn't even neat. Mr. French would not have been impressed.

The teasing subsided a few days later. Not once did I

think Michelle had said no for any reason other than that I was a boy.

My time at Guardian Angels was coming to an end. Boys left the school after grade four and usually headed for Iona, where they'd do both middle and high school.

"You know what, Robert?" my brother Michael said when we were talking about it at home one day.

"What?"

"You know what they do at Iona if you spit on the ground?"

"What?" I asked, starting to worry.

"If you spit on the ground there, one of the seniors makes you get down on your hands and knees and lick it up."

Michael started licking the air like it tasted nice.

"Do they really?" I asked.

"Yep," Gary said. "I saw it happen just the other day. Grade-five kid had to lick up his spit from the quadrangle. Those seniors, they'll push your face right into the ground to make sure you lick up that spit."

Michael and Gary took great delight in seeing how much this terrified me. I couldn't stop thinking about it. Any school that would make someone lick up their own spit—lick it up off the actual ground—must be really tough.

The funny thing was, I was not the kind of kid who ever, in a thousand years, would even think about spitting on the ground. I knew Dad would be most displeased if I ever did something so crude. I don't know why I was so worried.

Off to Iona I went, half expecting to see kids on all fours licking up spit. I'd survived my first four years of school, hadn't scared the girls too much, and was about to make my way in the big school down the road.

Surely it couldn't be that bad, I thought.

And it wasn't.

It was worse.

15

The Angry Asphalt

My elementary school was the tiniest of midgets, compared to the giant that was Iona.

Even I could walk from one end of my old elementary school to the other in four minutes. Iona seemed like a huge raging monster in comparison. In the middle was the quadrangle—an ocean of angry asphalt roiling in the summer heat. Around it was a hodgepodge of classrooms, a hall, a library, a tiny chapel, a science block, a manual arts workshop, and more classrooms. They, in turn, were surrounded by a great green moat of sports fields. Guardian Angels was so small you could have lifted it up and plonked it on the Iona quadrangle without hitting a building on any side. Lots of familiar faces came with me to start grade five, including David and Robert F, plus a heap of new kids too. In grades five to seven we had our own classrooms, our own lunch area, our own teachers, and our own deputy principal—our own little world inside the bigger school. Even so, I went from a school with a few hundred students to one that had nearly a thousand. It was still all new and gigantic and grand and frightening.

Everyone was trying to fit in at the new school, including me. I was desperate to find my place, to work out where I fit. Maybe it would be a new start. Maybe I'd be able to prove myself in the classroom. I was reading lots and could pick up facts fast enough that I didn't always need to work hard to understand them. Surely this would be a big advantage, I thought. Surely the other kids couldn't help but see how smart I was. It didn't work out quite the way I planned it, though. It turned out that other kids could pick up facts quickly too. Plus, they worked harder at it.

I'd only been at Iona a few weeks when a kid I'd never met before called me "Toe Nose." He must have seen the media coverage of my big operation when I was four and known that the doctors had made me a nose out of a toe.

Four weeks in I was being called half a dozen names that

weren't Robert—cripple, spastic, legless, and the dreaded Toe Nose. Even though some of my friends had come to the new school as well, sometimes it felt like the loneliest place in the world.

I'd pick up a new nickname every six months or so. Some would go out of fashion, to be forgotten for a year or two, and then come back in vogue. Some would slowly lose their power to hurt me and would fall into disuse. Quite quickly I had accumulated enough nicknames to last a lifetime. Counting down, here's my top ten.

Number 10: Toothpick Legs

Origin: A quick look at my legs and an assumption they were made of wood.

Originality: Medium.

Hurt factor: Mostly I was annoyed having to explain that my artificial legs were not made out of wood, thank you very much. They were made from fiberglass, metal, and rubber. Wood is so mid last century.

Laugh factor: Low.

How I got over it: Like a predator flourishing while its prey is plentiful, this nickname burned strong for a short while but came to an end after kids realized it didn't hurt, and got cranky when I yelled at them, "They're not made of wood!"

Number 9: Flat Nose

Origin: People opened their eyes and looked at me.

Originality: Low.

Hurt factor: Medium.

Laugh factor: Low.

How I got over it: One day I realized that for the first few years of my life I didn't have much of a nose at all. Hence the ancient proverb: "Better a flat nose than none at all."

Number 8: Pinocchio

Origin: *The Adventures of Pinocchio* was a children's story

written by Carlo Collodi in the 1880s. Pinocchio was carved out of wood and became a real boy, but not before numerous trials, including seeing his nose grow longer every time he lied.

Originality: Medium.

Hurt factor: Medium to low, especially once I remembered that my nose was squat and squashy, not long and pointy.

Laugh factor: Medium.

How I got over it: I told myself that I was a real boy, not a puppet made of wood, and that my nose would never grow.

Number 7: Go-Go-Gadget Rob

Origin: *Inspector Gadget* was an animated series about a bumbling detective that started in the early 1980s. He had all sorts of attachments connected to his body—a helicopter that came out of his hat, robot arm extenders, and bouncy springs in his legs that made him really tall really fast.

Originality: Medium.

Hurt factor: Low.

Laugh factor: Medium to high. It was kind of funny, after all.

How I got over it: People started to realize that my legs didn't actually have gadgets attached to them.

Number 6: Ugly Face

Origin: A not unreasonable reflection on what I looked like at the time.

Originality: Medium.

Hurt factor: Medium.

Laugh factor: Low.

How I got over it: It was too boring to care about for long.

Number 5: Retard

Origin: From the Latin *retardare*, meaning "to slow down," and, ultimately, *tardus*, meaning "slow." "Retardation" was used as a medical term for quite a long while, and it was a short step to label a person a retard.

Originality: Low.

Hurt factor: Medium.

Laugh factor: Low.

How I got over it: This one held a lot of power over me for quite a while. Yes, I had an ugly face and no legs, but my brain worked quite well, thank you very much. I just had to disconnect the dots for the people who thought that being physically disabled automatically meant you were intellectually disabled too.

Number 4: Transformer

Origin: The Transformers were a series of toys first brought out in the mid-1980s by Hasbro. They were robots that changed into cars (and motorcycles and planes and trucks) and then changed back again.

Originality: High.

Hurt factor: Low. This nickname was often used with affection and sometimes accompanied by the theme song from the TV series. Probably my favorite of all the nicknames

I got in school. Seriously, what young boy doesn't want to be a robot with guns built into his arms and the ability to change into a Mack truck or a jet plane on demand?

Laugh factor: High.

How I got over it: I didn't really need or want to get over this one, but it fell out of use.

Number 3: Stumpy

Origin: Well, yes, I had below-knee amputations on both legs and the part remaining after that surgery is called a "stump." How very observant of you.

Originality: Medium.

Hurt factor: Medium.

Laugh factor: Low.

How I got over it: I figured it was true, so ultimately there wasn't much to be done about it.

Number 2: Cripple

Origin: From the Old English *crypel*, meaning "to creep."

Originality: Medium.

Hurt factor: High. It was the mean truth of this nickname that hurt the most. It was so broad it seemed to cover all the very worst things I sometimes thought about my disability and myself. Plus, say it out loud and listen to how it sounds. Awful.

Laugh factor: Low.

How I got over it: "Cripple" was once a legitimate medical term, like "retard." In the 1800s and early 1900s, doctors used it to describe anyone who had difficulty walking. It's considered impolite now to say that someone is crippled—most people use the word "disabled" instead. I made my peace with this nickname by telling myself that it was technically valid, at least in the original medical sense. I decided that I wouldn't let this word have any power over me.

Number 1: Toe Nose

Origin: Journalist Hugh Lunn had written about the doctors at Mater hospital and how they had used bone and cartilage from my amputated toes to make me a new nose. Some bright spark read about it and then connected the dots.

Originality: High.

Hurt factor: High. Calling a six-year-old kid with glasses "four eyes" might be very hurtful and painful, but at least in some way it makes them a part of a group. There are lots of kids with glasses. They're not alone. They belong. Most kids just want to belong. They want to be one of the tall kids, one of the pretty kids, one of the fast kids, or the ones who are good at football. Or whatever. But Toe Nose was so specific. It cut to the very heart of me, making me ashamed of the good work the doctors had done. Sometimes I even wished they hadn't bothered. And it didn't apply to anyone else. I owned it. At the time it felt terribly hurtful, terribly strange. Who else had a nose made out of a toe? How do you defend yourself against that when someone is using it to tease you?

Laugh factor: None.

How I got over it: I never did get over this one. To this day, it's the one nickname that has any real power over me—the power to hurt.

16
Fitting In

I was smarter than some of the kids in the class—but not the smartest. I liked to watch sports—but couldn't really play any. I enjoyed listening to music—but I couldn't play an instrument. It didn't seem like there was any way to define myself other than by what was missing—my legs—and the strange extra I had: a nose made out of a toe.

A few weeks after I started at the new school, I was given a chance to distinguish myself. One of the priests who taught at the school turned up at our classroom door and talked to our teacher for a minute, then started taking students from the classroom three at a time. I was in the second group, so I didn't have a chance to find out what was going on when the first group returned fifteen minutes later.

"Robert, Matthew, Paul, please go with Father," our teacher said.

We were taken outside, downstairs, and into one of the wide grassy areas at the back of the school.

"Sit in a circle, please," the priest said.

I had no idea what was going on and started wondering if we'd done something wrong.

"Okay, boys, you're here to audition," he said. "As director of the junior choir, I'm listening to all the new students this week to assess their talent."

This should be fun, I thought.

Matthew went first. The priest gave him a piece of paper with the words to a hymn on it and asked him to sing. Then he asked him to sing some scales—up, down, up again. Then, for good measure, he asked him to sing the first few lines of the national anthem.

"Good, Matthew," he said. "Good."

He made some notes on a sheet of paper, turned to Paul, and ran through the same routine. More nodding. More notes.

Then he asked me to sing.

Everything sounded fine, in my head. I was a bit quiet at first, nervous, but I built up the volume as I hit the second verse of the hymn. Father had closed his eyes when I started singing but opened them again suddenly.

He tilted his head and curled the corner of his lip into a strange shape. I faltered for a second, but he waved to me to keep going. My voice went up and got crackly, then it went off-key.

"Just try to hold a note—any note—steady."

I settled on a tone I thought matched my speaking voice but couldn't hold it for long. The poor priest grimaced. I looked at the other kids. Matthew looked slightly disturbed. Paul was trying not to laugh.

I started the national anthem, but the priest waved his hand quickly in front of my chest. If there was a more universal sign for stop, I had yet to encounter it. He looked at me.

"Robert," he said, and then paused for what seemed like an eternity, "you're free to go."

I was already convinced I wouldn't find a place on any of the school sporting teams, and now it looked like choir was out of the mix too.

A few months later we were told we were about to head off on a big adventure—school camp.

Our camp that year was at Tallebudgera Creek on the Gold Coast. The campground was nestled between the beach, a creek, and the highway. It was only an hour and a half from Brisbane, but for a boy whose time away from home had been spent mostly in a hospital, it felt like a whole other world.

Camp was a combined outing for grades five and seven, designed so us new kids could spend time with some of the older boys. We weren't given any say in whom we bunked with and I didn't know too many of the kids in my hut.

I didn't even realize until we were on the bus and making our way noisily south that there'd be a whole group of unfamiliar boys who would see me with my artificial legs off for the first time. I figured they'd probably know I didn't have real legs—they would have seen me around the playground or maybe heard about it from someone else. Staying together in a hut would be different, though. It meant dealing with my disability in ways that were quite real.

Every day when I arrived home from school, I'd bolt up the stairs as fast as I could, hobble through our front door, sit on the couch, and rip off my artificial legs because they'd gotten sore. They came off before my school uniform, before I had a snack, before I switched on the television. Other kids came home and threw their schoolbags in the corner. I threw my legs.

I had taken them off and put them on in front of family, in front of friends, in front of doctors, but never really in front of strangers. Especially other kids I didn't know well. But at camp I'd be doing that every morning and afternoon.

When we arrived at Tallebudgera we scampered off the bus, grabbed our sleeping bags and clothes, and walked across the patchy grass to the shabby huts that were home for the duration. We waited nervously as the teacher opened the door for us, then peered inside.

There were bunk beds against all four walls and a nest of them in the middle. There were no windows except for a thin strip above one of the bunks. Beside the beds were tall, thin cupboards in which to stow our gear. It wasn't luxury, but for four days it would be our kingdom.

The kingdom, however, lacked secret places. The bunk beds all faced each other. There was nowhere to hide. The boys I hardly knew would be able to see me as I took off my legs and put them back on again. I chose a bottom bunk across from the door and plonked down my gear.

That first night, worried about taking my legs off in front of the others, I took my time wandering back from dinner. Of course that meant most of the other kids were already there when I arrived. I sat down on the bed and watched the other kids change into pajamas, swapping random camp tales. I held my breath and slipped off my legs.

No one saw me! Until I dropped my legs on the concrete floor.

At home, I'd take my legs off in the living room and leave them near the television.

There was carpet there. It didn't make much noise.

The design of my left leg had changed, and the metal poles and clump of metal for a foot had been traded in for fiberglass. When I took them off, both legs were just hollow fiberglass tubes. Dropped on the hut's concrete floor, they clanged and clattered like leg-shaped drums. Conversation in the hut stopped and everyone looked at me.

"Sorry," I said.

A few of the kids laughed, but most just went back to talking. There were bigger issues to deal with, like how to hide our contraband candy and stop other kids from stealing it. I faded off to sleep and dreamed of a kid stealing my legs and using them as bongos.

We spent our four days at camp doing camp things. We'd wake in the morning, grab our bowls and cups, and make our way to the big dining hall. After breakfast we'd take a short walk through the forest down to the creek and back again, followed by team-building games.

Afternoons we swam in the creek or sometimes in the surf, then wound down before a dinner of steak with steamed carrots and peas one night and chicken with steamed carrots and peas the next. After dinner, we'd wash our dishes and gather to watch the least offensive movie the teachers could possibly find. We'd sit in a small hall with a rickety projector showing some family-oriented fare on a white pull-down screen. Normally the films had talking dogs or kids who were younger—but already smarter—than us. The worst movies had both.

We were usually done by 8:30 p.m. and sent to get ready for bed and lights-out. At the end of the first night's movie, one of the teachers stood at the front of the hall.

"I have good news," he said.

Maybe we were going to watch a movie without talking dogs tomorrow night, I thought.

"On Wednesday night, instead of watching a film, we're going to have a talent show."

There was a confused and disappointed silence.

"It will be fun," he said.

"What do we have to do, sir?"

"You might want to put on a little skit or a scene from a play," he said. "Or maybe you can do magic tricks. Here's an opportunity, if you're not very sporty, to show us your stuff. You need to decide what to do by tomorrow afternoon and we'll give you some time to practice. Make sure you're ready."

Silence gave way to grumbling. We had not been warned we'd have to perform. No one in my hut had any ideas that night and we moved on to discussing more important issues of state before sleep.

The next day, we woke up and swarmed to breakfast. Around the breakfast table we started discussing some options.

"Let's just do something funny," one kid said.

"Yeah, yeah. That would be great."

Everyone nodded. Then one of the older kids, Paul, turned to look at me.

"Robert, can't you do gymnastics or something?" he asked.

"Gymnastics? No," I said.

"Yeah, you know, handstands and stuff?" Paul asked.

"Oh, yeah."

I'd told the other kids that I couldn't really do any sports but was okay at handstands. Cassandra and I did them all the time when we were playing.

"Why don't you do some handstands as part of our show?"

"What, in front of everybody?" I asked.

"Sure, why not?" Paul said.

"Onstage?'

"Sure."

Not only would it mean having my legs off in front of teachers, my grade-five classmates, and kids in grade seven, I'd also have to perform.

I said the only thing I could possibly say: "Ummm, okay."

It was settled. The act for our hut would be me getting up onstage and doing a handstand with my artificial legs off in front of the whole camp.

That afternoon we had time for practice and I found a patch of grass to try my handstands. A handstand requires strength in the arms to hold yourself up, strength in the torso to hold yourself steady, and strength in the hips to hold your legs still. Stumps instead of proper legs meant I had a lower center of gravity. That kept me stable and allowed me to stay upside down longer.

I took my prosthetics off and, with the other boys watching, I hoisted myself up on my hands. For a moment, I held myself still, then revealed my special trick—walking on my hands. I took a few steps forward and then gently lowered myself to the ground. At home it was easier, because I was letting gravity drag me down the hill, but I'd still only ever walked four or five steps in a row before.

The other boys were quiet for a few seconds.

"Well, it looks like we've got our act," Paul said.

The night of the talent show we ate dinner and tumbled into the hall, ready for some entertainment. We sat down, row after row of small boys in our shorts and T-shirts, messy hair and messy smiles, not really knowing what to expect. I hoped I'd have time to work up my nerve, but our hut was told that we'd be second up. I wondered if anyone would think to confiscate my legs if I got up and tried to run.

The first act was two kids doing card tricks. The last trick was just them throwing all the cards in the air. It didn't seem very magical, but it got a good laugh. Then it was my turn.

I took off my legs and gently lowered them to the floor at the side of the stage. Suddenly I was onstage with my legs off and dozens of kids staring at me. There wasn't much set-up required, so I planted my hands on the stage and pushed myself up. I locked my shoulders and elbows and hips into place and steadied myself. Blood rushed to my head.

I held myself there for a few seconds, staying steady, then decided to walk on my hands across the stage. The audience gasped when I took my first few steps. Once I was moving, it was actually easier to keep going than to stop and stay still again. So I kept going.

About halfway I started to overbalance and swung my legs backward to keep from tipping over. I regained my balance and kept going—six steps, seven. It was farther than I'd ever walked on my hands, even when I had gravity on my side going downhill at home. I was starting to feel confident that I could reach all the way over the other side. I sped up a little. My arms were aching, but moving faster meant switching from one to the other sooner. Nine steps, ten steps. I craned my head forward a little and realized I was really close, only a few more steps to go.

At step twelve I planted my right hand down on one of the playing cards strewn across the stage by the previous

act. It slid across the floor and I started to fall forward. I decided I'd made it far enough. I flung my legs back and came down from the handstand fast enough for it to look like it had all been planned that way. I turned and looked at the audience.

Silence for a few seconds. Then everyone broke into applause and loud cheering. I sat there on the stage for a few seconds, enjoying the moment.

At the end we voted on which hut had given the best performance, and the kids gave due consideration to the juggling acts, the joke-tellers, the card tricks, and me.

And we won. We weren't showered with trophies or prize money, but we did each receive a chocolate bar, which was even better, as far as I was concerned. Maybe taking my legs off wasn't that much of a big deal after all.

I enjoyed a kind of grudging respect for a few weeks after that, but the name-callings of cripple and Toe Nose eventually found their way back to the playground.

Then my parents told me they had a plan that might just help change everything.

17

Planning for Pretty

One Saturday morning after cartoons and Corn Flakes my parents sat me down at our kitchen table and told me about a new operation the doctors had planned.

"The doctors want to do some more work on your face," Mom said.

"Okay," I said.

"Now that you're older, the doctors have an opportunity to work out what you might look like as an adult," she continued. "They can make some small adjustments that they think might have a big impact on how you look."

I nodded.

"And in another three or four years, they'll need to do

further surgery that will make you look a lot more normal," she said.

Dad looked up from drinking his cup of tea.

"The doctors say they need to do this operation to prepare for that big one," he said.

"Okay," I said again.

I still had plenty of medical appointments. There was the orthodontist to see, and I needed new legs made every nine months or so as I outgrew them. But it had been years since I'd had an operation.

I'd spent so much time at the hospital that up until I was about twelve, I had the largest single file of any patient at Mater Children's Hospital. Ever. Then, either because I was getting too big a head about it or it was too bulky to actually file, or because it was too heavy to carry around anymore, the hospital split my file in two. I was a bit annoyed about it. All those appointments and operations, all the time spent sitting and waiting—and the one major achievement I had to show for it was being taken away. Somehow I'd fancied myself getting an entry in the *Guinness Book of World Records* someday. "Largest hospital file on record: Mr. Robert Hoge of Brisbane, Australia, with a file two thousand pages long and weighing in at eleven pounds." Then I was robbed by a technicality.

Detailed memories of my operations had faded. I was left with vague memories of the cold smell of antiseptic and ammonia, and bright surgery lights burning into my eyes as I counted backward from ten. I'd been too young when I had my big operations to remember the before-versus-after, the dramatic transformation. No, the memories I had were of the pain from being cut open, chopped up, and sewn back together.

My parents went on to explain the operation in detail. The doctors were going to remove a chunk of cartilage from one of my right ribs and use it to rebuild my face, they said. Cartilage isn't as strong as bone, but it can be easily shaped.

"Will it hurt?" I asked.

Mom wavered for a second.

"No operation is ever easy, Robert," Dad said. "You know that. But it's for the best."

They talked for a bit longer, told me more about what was involved. At no stage did they ask me whether the operation should be done. I don't know what I would have said. Instead, they asked whether I understood.

"Yes," I said.

The surgical team scheduled the operation for the last week of grade five, so I would be well and truly recovered for Christmas, which falls in the Australian summer, just after the end of the school year.

One lunchtime I sat chewing a ham and cheese sandwich and talked about the operation with one of my classmates, Matthew.

"Maybe no one will recognize you when you come back to school next year," Matthew said.

I hadn't even thought about that. My parents had mostly talked about minor changes.

"Maybe," I said.

"But if they're going to do a big operation, they'll have to *improve* how you look."

I shrugged, but it sounded like a good plan to me. My face was still a changing canvas, painted on, and over, by everyone except me. Every time I looked in the mirror I was reminded not only of just how far from normal I was but how little ownership I had of my face. I started to wonder just how much they could do with the operation. Maybe they'd fix the dents in the sides of my head, or make my nose look a little less squished. Perhaps they would smooth out some of my bumps and make me look not quite so Robert-like. Maybe after the operation kids wouldn't call me names so much.

The more I thought about the operation, the more I wondered how much difference it would make to how I looked. My parents kept saying it was only a small thing, but as the big day got closer and closer I couldn't stop thinking about it.

Finally it was time to head to the hospital. I'd had so many operations, the routine was still familiar. My parents would pack a few clothes into a bag. I'd add some toys and some books. We'd hop in the car and take the drive to Mater, where I'd be admitted and see some familiar old faces and lots of new ones. I'd usually come in a day or two before the procedure so doctors could check me out and make sure I was fine to be operated on.

After I was admitted, I settled into my usual bed, said good-bye to my parents for the night, and thought about how different I might look in just a few days.

Next morning it was showtime!

Morning operations were the best, because you weren't allowed to eat for hours and hours beforehand. Having an operation in the late afternoon meant having to skip breakfast and lunch.

I couldn't eat food, but I snuck a small sip of water from Mom and she sat beside my bed and read books to me while we waited. Eventually a nurse came and said it was time to get ready. I changed out of my pajamas and into a special gown. Then I was wheeled into surgery. I waited outside for a few minutes, where I was given an injection that made me sleepy.

Then I said good-bye to Mom and Dad and was wheeled through two big doors. The operating room smelled like a super-clean bathroom and was just as bright. It was full of odd machines and doctors and nurses in masks and gowns. I would have panicked, but the injection was already starting to make me feel groggy.

When I reached the center of the room, one of the doctors put a mask over my face and asked me to count backward from ten.

"Ten," I said.

All I could see above me were four bright lights. The lights pulsed like an octopus slowly opening its tentacles.

"Nine," I said. It was getting darker. The tentacles were getting ready to wrap around me. "Eight." Almost covering me now. "Seven."

Then I was unconscious. Claimed by the dark. The surgery took several hours. The team removed some cartilage from my ribs and partially rebuilt the bridge of my nose. They used leftover pieces to smooth out some other small gaps and bumps in my face and prepared it for the next operation in a few years. That would be the big one, the one that would make me look more normal.

A few days after the operation, the doctors were ready to take off the bandages. My parents were with me as they slowly unwrapped my head. They said I would be puffy and bruised, that it would take a while before we could see the differences. When I looked at my face in the mirror, the first thing I saw was my nose—big and bulbous. The same as it had always been. I couldn't see any change. My face was still just my face. I'd hoped to return to school after the holidays as a stranger, making my classmates wonder who the new kid was. That wasn't going to happen.

As part of the operation, I had splints stuck in my nose. A few weeks later they were due to be taken out. We arrived at the hospital midmorning for what should have been a simple procedure, but when the doctors tried to remove the splints they discovered tissue had grown around them.

Actually, I was the one who discovered it when they first tried to remove them.

The doctors had squeezed the top of my nose and gently tried to work the first splint loose. Pain shot through my nose and across my cheeks. It was like they were cutting my face open from the inside out. I screamed so loudly that Mom couldn't take it and had to go outside. Dad stayed with me and winced with my every scream as they tried again and again. One way or another, the splints had to come out. The longer they remained in, the more tissue would grow.

The doctors and nurses conferred in the corridor for a minute and decided they would put me under general anesthetic and remove the splints that way. Easy. Except I didn't want any of that. I was always ill after a general anesthetic and didn't want to brave the dark octopus again. After years of doing what I was told, I decided I'd take a stand.

I looked at Dad. "I don't want to go under general anesthetic," I told him.

"You sure?" Dad asked.

I nodded. "Let's just get it done," I said.

The doctors looked at Dad and he nodded. I tensed up as the doctors tried again. The pain was as bad as anything I'd ever felt in my life. But I bit down on my tongue and closed my eyes and tried not to scream as they pulled out the splints along with the tissue that had grown over them. Blood poured out of my nose and I almost blacked out. But it was done.

Sixth grade was much the same as fifth—games in the playground, unsuccessfully searching for a sport to play—until our elementary school rugby league coach, Mr. McConnell, let me help out "coaching." Teams would square off when trials were under way and he'd watch to see how well various kids played. I walked alongside and took tallies of which players were making tackles and which kids were making big runs. Every now and then someone would come up to me and whisper, "Hey, Robert, put me down for a couple of extra tackles, would you?" For the kids I liked, I did.

That year we had the great spitball war of 1983. It started innocently, with a few boys removing the inside of their pens and screwing up pieces of paper to shoot at the ceiling. It rapidly escalated to a full-scale war. I tried to stay out of it, but two of the major combatants sat right behind me and I was quickly dragged in. We soon graduated to pieces of paper that were rolled up and chewed until they were sticky with spit, then shot out of a pen like cannonballs. The war lasted only a few days before we were found out and almost the entire class got a week's lunchtime detention that we spent not licking spit off the ground, but scraping spitballs off the wall. If we were tall enough, I bet they would have made us do the ceiling too.

18

Green Is Good

By the time I turned twelve and reached grade eight, I'd given up on the idea of playing a competitive team sport.

In high school, organized interschool sports moved from Friday afternoons to Saturdays. But we didn't escape compulsory sports altogether. On Tuesday afternoons we had to do what the school called "health and leisure activities."

At the start of the year we were offered a range of options. I gave it as little thought as possible and chose lawn bowls, a game I'd never played before. I had little idea what it really involved, but at least it had to be better than the made-up misfit sports we had to play in elementary school.

On the first Tuesday we rolled up to the Wynnum Ex-Services Bowls Club, located on the waterfront next to the local dump. Dad and I would go to the dump every now and then, and he'd let me scavenge for treasure—junk-hunting by the bay.

The objective of lawn bowls was simple. Players rolled their bowl—a heavy ball you could just barely hold in one hand—so that it ended up as close as possible to a smaller white ball, called the jack. This was slightly complicated by the fact that the bowls were designed to curve as they rolled.

Games were played on a grass field that was meticulously leveled and maintained so bowls could roll smoothly. Each green was divided into playing strips about 5 yards wide and 32 yards long. Players would stand at one end and roll their bowls toward the jack at the far end. You scored points by having your bowl end up closer to the jack than your opponents' bowls after they'd all been rolled.

The game had been around for centuries and had even been banned by an English king in the 1300s because too many people were playing it and neglecting their archery training. As we hopped off our bus, I started to wonder if the old men waiting to help teach us had originally taken up the sport as soon as the ban was lifted. At that time, lawn bowls was seen as a sport for older people, and all the volunteers that day were in their sixties and seventies. They were happy to talk to us young kids and get us on our way to our first game of bowls.

Balance was the first problem I encountered. Normally players would bend both knees and step forward as they released the bowl. My left leg had no knee, so that approach wasn't going to work for me. Instead, I stretched it out to the side and placed my left hand on the ground for extra support. This made it difficult to look up, and most of the time, instead of looking at the jack, I looked down at the ground. I wasn't much good to begin with, but I felt I understood what I had to do to get the bowl where it needed to go, at least in theory.

We had a volunteer who taught us the basics, and then we spent another half hour playing in teams. I was captain and was competing against a kid named Shaun Luck. Shaun was bright, smart, and quick-witted. He was the first kid in the class to be onto a new fad or get a new gadget. And he was very competitive.

Shaun and I treated our game like the grudge match of the century. Bowls went everywhere—short, long, wide, wider. I doubt I got any within five feet of the jack. But the weight of that ball made sense in my hand. It felt heavy enough for me to know I could send it down to the other end with force when needed, but light enough that I could deliver it with the finesse it deserved. It felt good, and I won.

"Rematch next week, Hoge," Shaun said. It was not a question.

"Sure thing," I said. "I'll beat you again then too."

I hardly thought about lawn bowls in the intervening week, but by Tuesday I was set to return to battle. When we arrived, we had a new volunteer trainer. He introduced himself as Frank Plant. Frank was a member of the nearby Wynnum Bowls Club but had come to the neighboring club to help out. We introduced ourselves, ready to get down to business. Shaun and I made sure we were together for the rematch, but it wasn't quite that easy.

"Okay," Frank said. "Let's have a look at how you bowl."

"It's okay, Mr. Plant," I said. "We learned all about it last week. We're ready to play now."

He looked at me for a second, then gave a crooked smile.

"Robert, isn't it?" Frank asked.

"Yes."

"First thing, Robert," he said. "Call me Frank, 'cause that's my name."

"Okay."

"Also, we're not going to play right away," he said. "You can't learn to bowl in just one week. There's a lot of technique to master."

Inwardly, I groaned. Shaun shrugged. We both figured, though, that if we knuckled down and pretended to focus on mastering new skills, it would be just like last week. We'd be competing in half an hour.

Frank watched a few of the other kids bowl and made some suggestions.

Then it was my turn on the mat. Frank looked me over as I took up my unusual stance. I stuck my right leg forward, knee bent, pointing in the direction I wanted the bowl to go. Then I swung my left leg in a big arc and planted it almost perpendicular to my right. That meant I was low to the ground and had to arch my back to have enough room to swing my arm and deliver the bowl. That forced me to put my left hand on the ground for stability. I looked like a human spider.

The bowl I delivered wobbled out of my hand and came to rest about as far from the jack as possible without ending up in the gutter. I looked up as I delivered the bowl and saw Frank watching intently.

"Send another bowl down, Robert," he said. I did. The result wasn't much better.

"Is there a reason you look at the ground when you bowl?" Frank asked.

"Not really," I said.

"Keep your head up," he said. "Keep your eye on where you want the bowl to end up."

I craned my head forward, eyes focused intently on my target. But watching my arm swing forward had become habit and my head started to drift down again.

"Eyes up!" Frank shouted, just as I was about to let the bowl go.

It shot off wildly, wobbling to an off-target finish. Behind me someone laughed.

"Try it again," Frank said. "And keep your eyes forward."

I forced myself to look straight ahead. The bowl left my hand clean and smooth. It rolled and rolled and I kept watching as it got closer to the jack. It looked as if it was going to land right next to it, but it turned late and overshot the mark by about three feet.

"Bloody brilliant, Robert!" Frank shouted.

Frank carried a few more pounds than he probably should have, but it gave his face a jolly look, especially when he'd shout out, "Good bowl!" or "Nice shot!"

The other kids took turns bowling, and Frank gave them feedback too. Some listened, but others didn't care much and just walked up to the mat and hurled the bowl down. We spent the rest of the afternoon taking turns delivering bowls with Frank offering suggestions for improvement. It was a big help for me and I could already feel I was getting a better sense of the basics.

About twenty minutes before we had to pack up and return to school, Shaun shouted out to Frank, "Are we going to have a quick game? We need to have a rematch from last week."

"Not today," Frank said. "There's more practicing to be done. Maybe in a few weeks."

Shaun turned and looked at me. "Well, I don't want this guy next week."

But I knew I did.

We'd turn up at the Ex-Services Bowls Club every week and bowl our hearts out for an hour or so before we were packed back onto the bus and sent home. I'd seek out

Frank as often as I could for extra coaching, even when other kids were getting straight into a game.

One day Frank pulled me aside.

"You like playing lawn bowls, don't you, Robert?" he asked.

"Yep," I said.

"Would you like to come down to my club on Saturday, maybe meet one of the coaches and be assessed for disabled bowling?"

I didn't even know there was a special category for disabled bowling.

"I'd love to," I said. "I'll ask my parents about it." Frank gave me a thumbs-up.

Mom and Dad liked the idea, so the next Saturday we went to Wynnum Bowls Club, which was just across the road from the tennis club where Catherine played. I introduced Mom and Dad to Frank, and we set up to bowl. Frank had brought along Peter Reid, one of the club coaches, and they watched me bowl, made suggestions, and chatted to each other for about two hours. Like Frank, Peter was impressed with how I bowled, given my stance and my habit of staring at the ground while I delivered my bowls.

At the end of the session, Frank and my parents talked.

They thanked him for the extra effort he was putting in with me.

"I'm seventy now and didn't have too much to look forward to," he told them. "Doing this for Robert has given me a revived interest."

Now I was playing lawn bowls every Tuesday and Saturday. The Saturday sessions gradually became more important, with Frank and Peter trying to improve my swing and delivery. My stance remained a problem, though. Even with my left leg stretched out beside me and one hand on the ground, I wasn't stable. They decided I needed some sort of support, something that would give me a closer to normal stance and provide stability. Frank said he had an idea that would sort it out.

A few weeks later, he turned up with a metal stand his son had made especially for me to lean on as I bowled. It was thin, with padding on the bottom so it didn't damage the grass on the green, and almost three feet high. It was an immediate help. I was more stable when delivering a bowl, and it was much easier to keep my eyes focused where they needed to be.

After that, there was no stopping me.

I'd turn up for coaching on Saturday mornings and

spend hours listening to Frank, refining my technique, and trying again and again. Frank would stand ten feet or so in front of me as I delivered a bowl. Each time, he'd scoop the bowl off the ground and roll it back to me.

"That's good, Robert. Try to keep your arm parallel to your leg," he would say.

"Good bowl, Robert. But try to lock your elbow, and bowl from the shoulder."

"That's a good bowl, Robert. Now try to release the bowl closer to the ground, so it rolls out of your hand smoother."

"Good bowl, Robert. But don't look at me when you bowl. Look straight ahead to where you want the bowl to end up."

"That's good, Robert. You gave your wrist a bit of a twist at the end, though, which is why it went off-course. Try to lock it steady, like your elbow."

"That's a good bowl, Robert. You've got your wrist locked in place, but now you're bending your elbow again."

That was Frank. Always with the advice and always with the "That's a good bowl, Robert," no matter what tweaks he wanted me to make. Over and over again, until it started to feel almost unnatural not having the weight of that ball swinging in my hand.

Frank would stand for hours in the hot Saturday sun, leaning over so he could get a good look at my stance, sometimes standing in front of me, sometimes behind, sometimes beside. He'd watch intently as I delivered bowl after bowl after bowl. I quickly came to realize all of this work was the price of playing a sport well. It was the price of what I'd wanted for so long. And I loved it.

Our family Saturday-morning routine was locked in. After breakfast we'd go to the butcher and then the fruit and vegetable shop next door. We'd then go to the Wynnum library, where my parents would wait patiently as I wandered among the shelves, hunting for new science-fiction novels to read. The rule each week was that I could check out as many books as I could carry in one hand. I had big hands. Then I'd be dropped at the bowls club, where I'd spend a few hours practicing with Frank.

On the last Tuesday before the Easter holidays, all the kids who did bowls headed down to the Ex-Services Club as usual and had our practice. It was good fun, and everyone was excited. Holidays were so close, you could smell them like a sizzling sausage on a barbecue.

As we were getting ready to leave, I saw Frank having a serious discussion with another volunteer. In fact, they were arguing. I inched a little closer, trying to pretend I wasn't listening.

"You shouldn't be interfering by taking him for special coaching sessions," the man was saying to Frank.

"That's rot," Frank said.

"You're here as a volunteer, and if he was going to get training, it should be here at Ex-Services, not your club."

Frank just walked off, and I didn't get to talk to him before we were rounded up and put on the bus to head back to school.

When I got home, I told Mom what I'd overheard. She said maybe I should have a think about whether I preferred to play on Tuesday afternoons or Saturday mornings with Frank.

"That's easy. I'd rather stay with Frank."

That evening Frank phoned to talk to Mom. He relayed a bit more of the argument and said he was very upset. He told Mom he would never go back to the other club. Mom told him she didn't want him to sever his ties with the club on my account, but he said he didn't care. Mom told Frank that as far as she and Dad were concerned, I had their approval to train with him, and how any of us spent our free time on weekends was no one else's business.

"You're clearly very upset about it all," Mom said to Frank.

"Yes, I am," he said.

"Well, after Robert told me a bit about what happened this afternoon, I asked him what he wanted to do and he said he wanted to stay with you, bowling on Saturday mornings."

I thought Frank must have been saying an awful lot to Mom on the phone, because there was a very long pause, but she told me when she got off the phone that he hadn't said anything for a bit and then replied, "Thank you. I'll sleep tonight now."

After that, more training. Every month or so, Frank would find another player from Wynnum to compete against me. I'd win an individual round every now and then, but not very often. But I got to see firsthand how the experts did it, with Frank looking over my shoulder, giving guidance the whole way.

I had been training for sixteen months when Frank looked up at me with a smile one day.

"Robert," he said, "I think you're ready."

"Ready for what, Frank?"

"Well, I've talked to the club, told them about all the

training you've been doing, and they've agreed," Frank said.

I still didn't know what he was talking about.

"They've agreed you can join a team and start playing in competition with the adults, if you think you're ready," Frank said.

The stand Frank's son had made for me and all the training I'd done meant I could play in normal competition, rather than signing up for disabled bowls.

"Wow," I said. I was finally getting the chance to compete in a team sport.

"So, think you're ready?" Frank asked.

"Abso-bloody-lutely," I said.

Frank laughed.

"Good," he said, and smiled. "I've already put your name down for next week."

19

Game On

For my first official game, Frank signed me up to be lead bowler in a team of four. That might sound scary, but it's not. The lead bowler is just the bowler who goes first. The fourth bowler, called the skip, is the one who's actually in charge. Pretty much everyone starts out playing in fours, and being the lead bowler is a nice, gentle way to begin.

My job was simple. All I had to do was draw two bowls as close to the jack as possible. The opposing teams would alternate as the lead, second, third, and fourth bowlers all took their turn.

The skip stayed at the other end and barked orders to his three teammates before they bowled. No matter what he said, no matter what kind of crazy, impossible-to-pull-off shot he told you to play, the only acceptable response was to yell back, "Yes, skip!" like you were in the army taking orders.

I'm sure there were a few club members still dubious about a skinny disabled kid playing, but the first bowl I sent down that day gently nudged the jack.

"Good bowl!" Frank cheered.

The second stopped on the line about a foot behind it. Further down the bowling order, things got a bit more complicated. By the time the skip started bowling, there were already twelve bowls on the green. Sometimes they had to draw their last bowl around an opponent's bowl. Sometimes they'd have to put a bit of force behind their bowl—to push one of their team's bowls closer to the jack or knock the opposition's bowl out of the way.

Sometimes they had to shoot the bowl as fast as they could at the target. This shot was called the drive. There was little finesse to it. It was pure brute force. And truth be known, it failed as often as it succeeded. Frank refused to teach me to drive. He thought it was overused, a tool for players who couldn't draw properly. I'd have plenty of time to learn it down the track, he said.

In midafternoon a bell rang and we stopped for a break. Men in their forties, fifties, sixties, and seventies all took off their hats and headed inside—and so did I. We ate cucumber sandwiches and drank cups of tea. It was hot, but I drank that tea and ate those sandwiches like I had magically aged and turned into my father. My team was ahead, but only just. The game could go either way. We returned to the green fifteen minutes later.

The rest of the afternoon was an up-and-down affair. Our opponents caught up to us and then pulled slightly ahead, but we fought back. Going into the final round, the scores were level.

I stepped up to the green and drew my first bowl. It stopped right in line with the jack, two or three inches in front of it. I watched as the opposing team's lead bowl rolled down the green. It was getting closer to mine. Just as I thought it was going to fall short, it nudged my bowl and ended up just in front. My next delivery was the last one I'd make in my first proper game. It had to be a good one. I planted my foot and the metal stand down firmly, to make sure I was stable, and focused on exactly where I wanted the ball to end up. Then I let it go.

At first I thought the bowl was going too fast, too far.

But it crept out wide and gently swung back in. It edged its way around my first bowl and the other team's bowl until it nudged the jack. Frank gave me a loud clap, and I smiled. We stayed ahead for the rest of the game and my team won. I headed home a happy sportsman.

I graduated from playing fours to triples and then to pairs. Pairs was my favorite because it meant getting to bowl your first two bowls, swap with the skip while they bowled two of theirs, and then come back and bowl another two of yours.

I enjoyed playing pairs with Frank most of all. He was a good player—not a champion, since his aim was going off a bit in his old age, but we'd have great fun. He'd offer good suggestions and encourage me to take some risks. They didn't always pay off, but it was fun trying. And Frank was the perfect coach, weighing up the odds, asking if I fancied my chances, and telling me to go for it. We probably lost more matches than we should have, but Frank saw them as an opportunity to learn, to stretch my arm.

I'd found my sporting home—on a team—and not playing any of the sports I originally thought I would. Once again, my disability had restricted my choices, but then driven me to new ones that seemed so much better than anything else could have been.

Soon after, the Queensland Lawn Bowls Association chose to officially allow junior members. This meant we could be formally recognized by the clubs, play in interclub pennant matches, and compete in regional and statewide competitions. I was quick to register, and Mom and I even went off into town for the first meeting to elect representatives and office-bearers.

The first major singles competition I played was a round-robin event on the first day, with playoffs on the second. Frank came with me and we settled in for what I'd decided was going to be a winning day. I cruised to an easy victory in my first match, and my second match looked just as simple. My opponent was a few years younger than me, smaller, and looked like he'd only been playing a year or two at most. A pushover, I thought.

Except the kid was good. I lost the first round four–nothing, the worst result possible. My opponent would draw a bowl within half an inch of the jack every time. Or if I drew shot, he'd give my bowl a nudge, knock it back three feet or so, and claim the round. Time after time, he kept taking the shot or denying me whenever I came close.

We broke for lunch in the middle of the game and I sat and chatted with Frank.

"Robert," he said, "I think it's time we taught you how to drive."

I shrugged, doubting that it would have made much difference that day anyway. I went back out there rested, focused, and determined to redouble my efforts. And got resoundingly beaten. Luckily, I won my third match and progressed to the finals the next day. I made it through the morning, but I was beaten in the semis and ended up in third place. But I got a trophy—the first I'd ever received for a genuine sporting achievement.

The next Saturday morning, I turned up for coaching and Frank had organized the club's driving expert to come down and teach me. He was a tall, fierce man and would drive his bowl down the other end of the green so fast that when it connected with another ball it sounded like it was splitting an atom. It was a good lesson, but I wasn't the best driver because I delivered the ball stationary. A lot of the best drivers "walked into it," but I was stuck standing on the mat.

In any case, I was happy with the skills Frank had taught

me. Happy he'd brought me into a competition, made me part of a team, showed me that it could sometimes be just as much fun losing as winning. So long as I was in a team. Preferably his team. Most people have a favorite sporting coach, a favorite teammate, and a favorite grandfather. Frank was all of those things to me.

I'd wanted so desperately to be part of a team. I'd wanted to be cheered when I got something right and jeered when I didn't. I wanted to win, and when I didn't, I wanted to lose with friends by my side. Lawn bowls gave me all that and more.

20

Growing Up Slow

Nowhere, ever, will you find a worse example of humanity than grade-nine boys. That included me.

At some stage that year a bunch of us decided that filling our mouths up with water at a drinking fountain and spitting it at our classmates was the coolest way we could spend our time. Extra points were awarded if you could squirt water over someone's shirt just before class resumed so they'd have to sit there, soaking wet, looking stupid.

At first we'd try to act casual, as if our mouths weren't full of water, but it was pretty hard convincing someone you weren't going to squirt water on them when you couldn't talk. Soon people began running after each other to deliver a mouthful. I was neither fast enough to run after people nor fast enough to escape when they came after me, so I got drenched. I sat with Robert F one lunchtime, just before class resumed, soaked in water.

"This is an issue that must be addressed," I said.

"What are you going to do?" Robert F asked.

"I've got an idea," I told him.

I'd spied an empty shampoo bottle of Mom's in the bathroom a few days earlier. It was long and slender, and small enough to fit into my pocket. I rinsed it out, brought it to school, and filled it with water. While I still didn't have the speed of the other kids, my weapon had a significantly better range.

This was a major escalation. It moved the fight in the quadrangle from one-on-one spit-and-run attacks to something more serious. For a few glorious days I had the upper hand. I'd hold the shampoo bottle by my side and squirt an enemy combatant as I walked by. Or I'd poke my head around the corner of a building and wait until I could squirt someone, then quickly duck back away, unseen. Then other kids realized they could do the same thing.

Next, some genius figured out that because the liquid we were squirting at each other was no longer carried in the mouth, it could be something other than water. There we were, filling up bottles with water and toothpaste and shampoo and squirting each other.

I took part, lest I get left behind in the arms race. My preferred concoction was about three parts water with a little shampoo and a dollop of toothpaste. It was the perfect combination. Not too thick, so it still got plenty of distance when squeezed out of the bottle, but tainted enough that if it hit, it stuck, leaving a coconut-smelling sheen topped with a minty-fresh zing.

The conflict attracted a lot more attention now that it was no longer just the occasional kid with water down the back of his shirt. The teachers' security council gave a few kids detention and we were all threatened with serious repercussions if the combat continued. Chemical warfare in the schoolyard was frowned upon.

The game was over.

One lunchtime I'd retreated to the classroom to escape the conflict and finish some math homework I hadn't done the night before. A few minutes later one of the other kids, Ben, came in too.

"Hey, Toe Nose," he said.

"Get stuffed, Ben," I said.

"Original," he said. "Original like your nose."

"You only just worked out that my nose is like this?"

"It's been obvious for a while," Ben said.

"No joke," I said.

"I don't know how you cope with a nose like that—it's all big and round and squishy."

"Really," I said. "Taken a look at your own nose anytime recently? It's pretty huge."

He did, in fact, have a rather large nose.

Ben scoffed something under his breath and walked out of the classroom. It wasn't the end of it as far as I was concerned.

Instead of finishing my homework, I grabbed an exercise book, ripped a page out and set about drawing a portrait of Ben. In profile. It wasn't the most lifelike portrait, but I absolutely nailed one part of it—his nose. It took up half the page, emerging from his face like a massive mountain. I colored in his hair, drew on ears and lips, but the nose got special attention—it was giant, pendulous, overpowering. I drew gaping nostrils, then held my artistic creation up and smiled. It was beautiful. But it was missing something, something to give it scale and put the size of the nose in context.

I drew several spaceships entering and leaving his cavernous nostrils, like they were docking at a spaceport. I titled it "Spaceport Ben" and slipped it into his desk. Proud of myself, I went to lunch and promptly forgot about it.

As with such things, though, a day of reckoning was to come. And it reckoned soon enough.

Later that week I was called down to see Mr. Fuller, the deputy principal. Most of the school lived in a vague, unspecified fear of Mr. Fuller. He was the perfect second-in-command. He delivered the bad news when needed and administered a strict, no-nonsense form of discipline that mainly worked by keeping students so in fear of the threat of getting in trouble that they behaved.

I had no idea what I was being called down for. What Michael and Gary had told me about discipline at Iona started and stopped at the consequences of spitting, not what happened when you were called to the deputy principal's office.

I sat waiting outside his office for a few minutes before I was called in.

He sat behind a big desk, papers neatly piled on one

side. On the wall he had shelves with books and sporting trophies.

"Sit down, Robert."

"Yes, sir."

"Do you know why you're here?" he asked. I wondered if it was meant to be like confession at church and I was supposed to say, "Forgive me, Mr. Fuller, for I have misbehaved. It has been about forty-two days since I last admitted to my bad behavior." Then I'd confess to talking in class, answering back to teachers, swearing, not doing my homework, and a range of other sins.

I settled for a simple "No, sir."

"I understand you and Ben have been having some disagreements," he said. "That there's been some teasing going on."

I relaxed. At least I wasn't getting in trouble, I thought. It was just teasing incident number 8,024 in a long line of teasing incidents. I knew there would be more. It hadn't had much impact.

"Well, sir, it wasn't anything, really. Nothing that got me very upset, anyway."

Settling scores in the deputy principal's office might seem like a good idea to some, but Dad had always taught me it was better to face things head-on. You might not always win, but getting someone else to fight your battles for you just encouraged more fights in the future.

Unfortunately, I'd misunderstood what Mr. Fuller was saying.

"It's fine that you didn't find it very upsetting, Robert, but that doesn't mean Ben didn't," he said.

It took a moment to sink in. I wasn't the teasee this time, apparently. I was the teaser.

"Oh, okay."

"Not really okay, Robert, no," he said. "I'd expect that you more than most boys would know how hurtful teasing can be."

"Yes, sir." I started to go red.

"Surely you know that it can be a very mean thing to pick on someone because of the way they look?"

"Yes, sir."

"Was there a particular reason for what you did? What you drew?"

I thought about that for a moment. "No, sir," I said. I made a note to never, ever draw anything again.

Even if the spaceships going in and out of the nostrils did look cool. And very funny.

"Well, Ben has been down here twice in the last two weeks, very upset. Don't do it again."

"Yes, sir."

Mr. Fuller waved me out the door and sent me away with no further punishment than my shame and having missed lunchtime.

I was genuinely surprised to learn how much my drawing had upset Ben, because I was teased so often myself, and I became better and better at dealing with it as I got older. Sometimes it wasn't just kids who were cruel, though. Sometimes it was adults, and somehow that was much worse.

In grade ten we had to do a week of work experience, to see what life was like in the adult world. I signed up to do work experience as a teacher. It was the default for a bunch of us. I didn't know why I chose it. I was pretty sure I didn't want to be a teacher, but it seemed as good a choice as any.

Come work experience week, another boy and I were shipped off to a Catholic elementary school I'd never heard of. The week before, we'd all been given a lecture about taking the opportunity seriously and behaving appropriately. When we turned up to the school, we were neatly dressed and minding our manners. The two of us went to the administration block and waited outside the principal's office for what seemed like ages. Then she came out, introduced herself, and told us that I would be working with the grade-seven class and the other boy would be working with the grade-two class.

At Iona, relief teachers, student teachers, and work-experience kids were all fair game for students to pick on, but the kids at this school were just fine. The kids in the classroom were smart and engaged, and the kids in the playground were well-behaved. None of them said a thing about my funny face or my legs. I got the occasional stare from a student here or there, but nothing I wasn't used to.

My biggest problem the whole week was correcting the grade-seven students' spelling in class and trying to work out whether the proper spelling was "potatoes" or "potatos" (hint: it's "potatoes"). The week sailed by and was capped off with a half-day Friday for us. I said good-bye to my grade-seven class and thanked the teacher who'd looked after me. Before I could go, though, I was sent to the principal's office. I thought maybe the other student and I were going to get a quick thank-you, but he was nowhere to be seen.

I waited outside the office for a few minutes before being called in. The school principal seemed nice enough. She was a well-spoken middle-aged woman who seemed popular with the students.

"It would have been appropriate," she said, without a hello, "if we were warned before you came."

I had no idea what she was talking about.

"Warned?" I asked.

"Yes, warned," she said. She raised her voice slightly, like I was a kid in grade two. "About you."

"About me?"

"When you arrived on Monday, we had to quickly swap the class you'd be in. You were supposed to work with the grade-two teacher."

I wondered for a second whether kids in grade two would be tested on how to spell the plural of "potato." My next thought was that until we'd arrived, we were just names on a piece of paper anyway, so it couldn't have been that hard to change. Then it dawned on me what she meant. She was talking about the way I looked.

I hadn't given any thought before I arrived to what the

younger kids might think of me. I doubt my teachers at Iona had either. I did okay there. Surely I'd do okay at another school. What was there to worry about?

I didn't know what to say.

I started to cry.

"I'm sorry," I said.

"Good," she said, and got up to open the door for me.

I cried all the way across the school oval to where Dad was waiting to pick me up. I did my best to compose myself before I hopped in the car, but he knew something was going on and asked what was wrong. I explained, and then pleaded with him not to get out of the car and go give the principal a piece of his mind.

"And don't tell Mom either, okay? I can handle it."

He thought about it for a minute, then decided it was up to me. "Okay."

It wasn't the last time I cried about the way I looked, but it was the very last time I apologized to anyone else for it.

21

The Choice

Okay, go find that imaginary clay baby's head sculpture you did. Any version is okay—pretty, ugly, or not-so-ugly. This is the last time you'll need it. Promise.

Imagine you've got this grand plan to give it one last big effort, to finish it off. You think about what you might do, start working out which tools you'll need and whom you can ask for help. Then someone goes and takes it away. You've spent ages working on it and now you'll never know how it would have turned out. How annoying would that be?

My doctors felt a bit like that. They were artists, and they didn't like leaving their work half-finished. They had done a tremendous amount of surgery on my legs and my face and had made a very important difference to my life. Now they wanted to finish their masterpiece.

I'd known for years that my surgeons wanted to do another major operation. This would be "the big one," they said—the operation that would make everything right. And one day, just after I had turned fourteen, I arrived home from school expecting to eat some snacks, watch some television, and begrudgingly start my homework, when my parents said the day had arrived. My doctors had discussed it with Mom and Dad, who in turn raised the prospect with me.

Most importantly, they told me, it would mean a massive improvement to how I looked.

"My last operation didn't make that much of a difference," I said.

"That last one was mostly about getting ready for this one," Dad said.

Mom nodded. "This one's a lot bigger, Robert."

"They're going to do a heap more work," Dad said. "Almost as much as you had with your first big operation when you were four."

My bumps would be ironed out, my nose would be

made almost normal, and my eyes would be moved slightly closer together. I would look much, much better.

By then I'd started to notice girls. And I'd started to notice girls noticing how I looked. I think my doctors were also starting to notice me noticing how girls noticed how I looked.

While the idea of another big operation had always been in the back of my mind, I hadn't really given it much thought. Now I wondered what it would be like to look normal. Would I feel different if I had a regular nose? Would girls notice me more if the dents at the sides of my head were filled in? Would other kids tease me less?

Would I still be called Toe Nose?

Over the next few weeks I asked my parents a question here, a question there. Then they sat me down and said it was time to talk properly. I wasn't surprised that they wanted to hear my opinion before they made their decision. They were good like that.

"Robert," Mom said, "you know we've been talking about you having another operation on your face. A big one."

"Yep."

She looked at Dad and took a deep breath. "Well," she

said, "this decision isn't up to us. You're fourteen, and we think you should decide whether the doctors do the operation or not."

"It's your life, so it's your choice," Dad said.

What? Had I heard my parents properly? Were they really asking me to decide if I should have an operation? And not just any old operation—a massive one that might make me look normal?

My breathing sped up. My heart pounded so loudly I could hardly concentrate. I realized that was exactly what they meant. I couldn't make a single one of the thousand thoughts racing around my head stay still for even a second. I panicked. Did I have to give them an answer right now? I had no idea what to think or even how to think it.

Mom must have noticed how worried I looked.

"We're not asking for your advice to help us choose, Robert," she said. "It's entirely up to you. And you don't have to decide right away."

"The doctors are really eager for the operation to go ahead," Dad said. "But like I said, it's your choice."

The surgeons understood that I had formed close friendships with my buddies, but I was entering that time the experts referred to as "the period when a boy will hopefully begin to form relationships with creatures known as girls."

They were sending Mom and Dad a clear message: "Robert has done very well in life. So far. He's survived childhood and made it into his teenage years. Now we need to prepare him to become a proper functioning adult."

The doctors wanted me to have a normal life. They wanted me to have girlfriends. They wanted me to grow up and fall in love and maybe get married and have children, like my friends would. And they thought all of that would be so much easier for me if I weren't so ugly.

They had been concerned about this right from the start. When I was first born, one doctor had examined me and told Dad that I'd have normal mental ability and hit puberty like every other kid, but be rejected by others because of the way I looked. At the time, Dad had a wife under sedation who couldn't bring herself to see the massively deformed baby she'd just given birth to. He had four other kids at home who needed looking after. He had a job he had to keep because he was the breadwinner in the household. And he had me. What might happen if I made it to puberty was the least of his problems back then. Fourteen years later, the question seemed much more important. I was a million light-years away from being ready to go up and ask a girl if she wanted to go out with me—not counting playground attempts in grade four—but I understood, if only in theory, why the doctors were worried.

My face still looked like someone had driven a train across it and left tracks behind as scars. I knew the routes they traced across my head. I knew where they disappeared beneath my hairline. I knew the bumps. I knew my nose was so wide I could see it out of the corners of both eyes. I knew my ugliness like—well, like it was my own face.

We started talking it through in more detail. How long would the operation take? I wanted to know. What would they be cutting up this time? Where would they move things to?

First, the easy part. Doctors would fill the gaps in my skull from previous operations. I had slight depressions at the front of my forehead and a massive crater on each side of my head, running down to my eyebrows. This work wouldn't be too hard. The doctors would simply find some more spare cartilage and I'd end up with a scar on the left of my chest, just like the one I had on the right.

Most of the work would be around my nose and eyes,

though. Doctors would un-squish my nose, and raise the bridge and narrow it, so it didn't look quite so much like a lump of clay that had hardened before it could be properly shaped.

Unfortunately, fixing my nose would also highlight the fact that my eyes were slightly wider apart than they should be. They were close enough to allow me to focus both eyes on the same thing, but they were still a little bit farther apart than was ideal. When I had a big, flat nose this wasn't quite so pronounced, but it would become obvious if the doctors fixed it. If they were going to fix one thing, they'd have to fix everything. And fixing it all would make me look much more normal.

Normal.

I'd had enough surgery as an older child to know that it was a lengthy, painful, distressing process, and that things could go wrong. But I'd also seen pictures of handsome men with symmetrical faces and proper noses—the kind of man girls found attractive, with a strong chin, chiseled jaw, and piercing eyes. They were on television all the time.

I was smart enough to know I'd always be outside of ordinary—no matter what the doctors did to my face, I would never go to sleep one night and wake up the next morning to discover I'd grown new legs—but I wanted to know what I'd look like after the surgery. I tried to imagine the new face the doctors would give me, thinking about what the operation could mean for my future. It all went around in my head for a few weeks: the pain, the risks, the uncertainty, and the awful, enticing thought of blending in.

Then, decision time.

Mom, Dad, and I sat at the kitchen table. Michael was there too, so he joined the discussion.

We sat around and talked in circles for a while, me and Mom and Dad and Michael. We guessed at what I might look like. We talked about how they'd do the operation at the end of the school year and hopefully have me back with my friends in January, new face and all.

"There are some risks involved, though?" I asked.

"Yes," Dad said.

My parents ran through them one by one. I could die on the operating table, a risk with all surgery. I could get an infection, which had happened before. It could mean more pain, more scars, and might even undo the work the doctors had already done. It might not work as well as everyone expected, with doctors doing hours and hours of work and me looking the same at the end. Or worse.

Mom pointed out that the doctors would be moving my eyes again. "If they damage the nerves around your eyes, there's a chance you might lose your eyesight," she said.

"Why can't they move one eye at a time?" I asked. "And be super careful?"

"It doesn't work like that," Dad said. "It's one operation, Robert. They have to do all the work at the same time."

Michael, who had mostly been quiet until then, suddenly piped up. "What use is looking pretty if he can't even see himself?"

I paused at that, and everyone turned to look at me. I still don't know exactly how or why, but that one question brought all of my thinking into focus.

In that instant I owned my face.

I could trust myself to the doctors who had done so many wonderful things to get me so far. I could give them the chance to move me a bit closer to normal, risks, rewards, and all. Or I could take my chances and make my ugly way in a sometimes ugly world just the way I was.

Until then, almost everything in my life had been governed by what I looked like. But I'd had no ownership of that. I'd had no say in my appearance and no control over what was decided in the name of my face.

When my brother made his comment, I suddenly understood what it really meant to make that choice for myself, to take ownership over my face.

I decided right then that I was not going to have that operation. I might never be a pretty sculpture, but I was done with being the doctors' clay.

I knew I was ugly. But everyone is uglier than they think. We are all more beautiful too.

We all have scars only we can own.

An operation to fix my face would mean leaving behind this horrid, bumpy, uneven, unequal, disquieting, disfigured, disturbing face that made me who I am. Sometimes people would say to me that I'd managed to do quite well despite my appearance and my disability. And I started to realize that I hadn't become who I was *despite* those things. There was just as much chance I had become who I was *because* of my ugliness and my disability.

"I don't want to have this operation," I told my parents. "I don't want to have any more operations. Ever."

It was me, my legs, and my ugly face against the world.

Me, age five, posing with one of my very first
pairs of prosthetic legs and an ugly T-shirt.

Learning to swim without legs was
difficult but worth all the hard work.

My neighborhood friends Evelyn (left) and
Cassandra and me, goofing around in my yard.

Handstands are a lot easier
when you don't have any legs.

My lawn bowls coach, Frank Plant, and me at the
Wynnum Bowls Club where I learned to play.

My dad, my sister Paula (back), and my sister
Catherine join me for a special photo on my
very first day of school.

Me showing my dad, Vince, the Olympic Torch, just before I set off on my part of the torch relay for the Sydney 2000 Olympics.

Mom and Dad with me several weeks after a really big operation I had when I was four and a half to make me a new face.

Brothers and sisters all grown up: (clockwise from back left)
Michael, Gary, Paula, me, and Catherine on the
front steps of the house we all grew up in.

One of my favorite places in my house.

If you look closely, you can still see the scars from many of
the twenty-four operations I had while I was growing up.

It's good to be able to laugh at yourself.
Especially when things go wrong.

When not playing around with it, I
use this old leg as an umbrella stand.

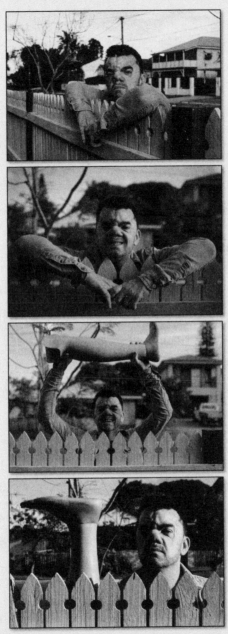

I enjoy longs walks by my front fence and
showing off one of my old prosthetics.

UGLY Q&A

Why did you want to tell your story?

Telling stories is pretty much the only thing I'm good at, so I thought writing down my own would be a good idea. I decided that talking about what it was like growing up different and how that influenced my life would be interesting to kids who sometimes feel a bit out of place themselves.

It's okay to be different, and it's really important for all of us to talk about how we're sometimes different from one another.

How do you define yourself?

In lots of ways. I certainly consider myself ugly, but I don't think that makes me mean or dumb or awful. It's just how I look. It's part of who I am and has affected my life in many different ways. I feel the same about my disability. Those aspects are only parts of my life, though. I also like reading and writing and traveling and taking photographs.

None of us is just one thing—we're all made up of many

parts. People who like softball might also like swimming and spelling. People who like football may also like computer programming and cooking.

Why did you choose to call your book *Ugly*?

Okay, did you read the answer to that last question or not?

I thought it was important to choose a title that got people thinking about what it meant to be different and how the way I look impacted my life. Plus, I knew I'd be writing the title a bunch of times, so choosing a short one seemed smart.

What's it like having prosthetics?

Good and bad and weird—often all at the same time. Imagine having a pair of shoes that are so tall they almost double your height when you put them on. Pretty weird, right? It would take a lot of work to balance properly on them. Sometimes they'd rub against your real legs and make them sore. You probably wouldn't be able to run very fast with them on or walk as far. That's what it's like for me wearing prosthetics.

But I can also choose what design my prosthetics are, and I get to have some say in how tall I am. They also let me move around much more independently than if I didn't have them, so overall I think it's a big benefit having them.

What are your favorite kinds of stories?

I've always loved stories about space, and action and adventure.

Is it better to speak politely or honestly?

Honestly. But politeness and honesty are not really opposites, are they? You can speak honestly without being mean.

What advice do you have for someone who is differently abled?

Oh, wow! There's probably a whole other book I could write in answer to that question. I think it's important to understand that, even if your circumstances and your set of abilities are unique to you, they don't necessarily have to define you. But you don't have to ignore them entirely, either.

It's okay if your physical abilities form a big part of what makes you who you are. Of course they probably will. But no one ability or disability is you.

What advice can you give for people speaking to someone who is differently abled?

First, don't be shy. Come and talk to us. You'd be surprised just how many other kids who are a bit different from you like soccer or video games or horseback riding or solving math problems.

Sometimes people will be okay with talking about themselves, and sometimes they won't. There's no easy answer for every person, but you'll figure it out over time. Just remember that every single one of us is made up of a bunch of different pieces. You make friends with people, not their disability.

At the end of the book you make a big choice about your future. Do you think your life would be different if you'd made a different choice?

Absolutely! I don't want to say too much in case you're reading this before reading the main part of the book (spoilers!), but I am who I am because of the sum of all the choices I've made in my life. Sometimes I wish I could run an experiment just to see what my life would have been like had I made a different choice. That would be cool.

But I still think I'd make the same choice, no matter what the experiment showed.

The choice I made sent me on a certain path. It didn't always seem like the easiest or smartest decision, but it got me here, writing this book, talking to you. So life is pretty good.

How did you deal with bullying?

The first thing I realized was that the kids who were bullying me were trying to take away my right to define who I was by doing it for me. By calling me cripple or stumpy or flat-nose, they were saying those were the only things about me that mattered.

So I dealt with the bullying by understanding that those kids didn't get to define me—only I got to define me. And my definition was a lot different from theirs.

You come from Australia. What's your favorite Australian animal?

Kangaroos, koalas, and crocodiles are all great. But my very favorite Aussie animal is a bird called a kookaburra. Kookaburras have a call that sounds like a crazy cackle. Trust me. Check out a video online and you'll see what I mean.

What is the most important lesson you'd like for readers to take from your story?

It's okay to be who you are. It's okay to be different. That difference is part of you, but it's not the only part of you.

Library Media Center
McCarty School
3000 Village Green Drive
Aurora, IL 60504
630-375-3407